INFORMAL SECTOR IN INDIA

INFORMAL SECTOR IN INDIA

S. Dharmaraj

ABHIJEET PUBLICATIONS
DELHI 110 094

ABHIJEET PUBLICATIONS
2/46 Tukhmeerpur Extension
Delhi-110 094
Phone: 011-22960492, 65698474
E-mail: abhijeetpublication@gmail.com

INFORMAL SECTOR IN INDIA

First Published 2007

ISBN 978-81-89886-42-4
(Price: Rs. 350/- INR)

PRINTED IN INDIA

Published by J.K. Singh for Abhijeet Publications, Delhi-110 094, Lasertypeset by Gaurav Graphics, New Delhi and Printed at Himanshu Printers, Delhi.

Dedicated

to

My Parents

M. Sengamalam

&

M. Kamalam

Preface

In India the conditions and quality of the life of informal groups are very miserable. Even though the government have launched various social security measures to safeguard the interests of these unorganised poor. They are unable to utilize it because of many loopholes in it.

This book narrates the social security measures, for the construction industry workers, agricultural labourers and other unorganised groups and also deals the synoptic book on informal sector. The main attention of both central and state governments is safeguard the interest of informalised sector like Beedi, quarry workers and other unorganised and non-institutionalised set up in the society.

S. DHARMARAJ

Acknowledgements

I am extremely thankful to T.A. Julius, Former Head of the Department of Economics, Nehru Memorial College, Puthanampatti for his support and encouragemenr throughout for writing this book.

I owe my sincere thanks to R. Manimekalai, Head of the Department in Economics, Nehru Memorial College, Puthanampatti for her timely help.

I am greatly indebted to Dr. V. Selvaraj, Reader in Commerce, Nehru Memorial College, Puthanampatti for his constant encouragement.

My special thanks to Dr. D. Kumar, Department of Economics, Jamal Muhammad College, Tiruchirapalli, Dr. S. Murugan, Department of Economics, EVR College, Tiruchirapalli and Mr. K. Palanivel, Prof. EVR College, Tiruchirapalli for helping me in all matters of the book information.

I take this opportunity to express my heartfelt thanks to my beloved colleagues P. Rasamahendran, Mr. M.R. Karuppaiah, A. Shanmugam, Dr. V. Murugesan for their constructive criticism in this work.

I owe my affectionate thanks to my beloved friends Mr. A. Sekar, Mr. K. Thiagarajan, Mr. V. Senthil Kumar for their enthusiastic help.

I feel happy to thank my in-laws Mrs. & Mr. A. Eswaran and Mrs. and Mr. Lakshmi Narayanan Software Engineer, Hyderabad, Mr. Murugapandian, Project Manager, Chennai and Mrs. E. Maithili, Lecturer Computer Science S.A. Engineer College, Chennai.

Without their constant pressure and cooperation, I would not have visited centres of learning for data collection.

I will be failing in my duty if I could express my profound thanks to my wife Mrs. Lalitha senior Lecturer in Chemistry, M.A.M. College of Engineering, Tiruchirapalli and to my sons Keerthivasan and Thiru Srinivasan for their timely help in bringing this book in time.

My profound thanks to my beloved sisters Jayalakshmi Muthukannu, Bhagyalakshmi and Umarani who helped me in many ways.

I owe my sincere thanks to my mentor Mr. S. Palanimuthu, M.A., B.Ed. (Retd. Teacher) and Mrs. Kamatchi for the moral support and financial support to take up this project.

I am thankful to Abhijeet Publications, New Delhi for their interest and cooperation in publishin this book.

S. DHARMARAJ

Contents

Contents

1

Social Security Measures in India

In recent times, the subjects on Social Policy specially "Social Security" have become increasingly more important in development discussions concerning the developing countries. The societies in these countries derived their support and sustenance from their time tested self-sufficient system, founded on the care of the individual by the family or the community. The household had been a compact basic unit and the social, cultural and economic life was based on mutual help. This fabric of village kinship started disintegrating with the social changes, the pressure on land and the process of industrialization. The growth of trade and commerce in urban area and increase in employment opportunities in the in employment opportunities in town and cities initiated migration of people to urban areas. This rural-urban shift had two-fold effect. Firstly, it eroded the homogeneous character of the rural community; and secondly, it brought about the need to provide an alternative form of social security in the changed environment. The disintegration of joint family system, migration of people from rural to urban area, and the inhomogeneous character of the society made the subject more important. In fact a feeling has developed that the development problems could primarily be solved by improving or setting up an appropriate "social security" system.

What is Social Security?

There is no commonly accepted definition of the term social security. The International Labour Organisation has defined social security as "The security that society furnishes, through appropriate organization against certain risk to which the members are exposed. These risks are essentially contingencies against which the individual of small means and meagre resources control cannot effectively provide by his own ability or presight or even in private combination with his fellows, these risks being sickness, maternity, invalidity, old age and death. It is the characteristics of these contingencies that they imperil the ability of the working men to support himself or his dependants in health and decency".

The ILO definition of social security includes two main elements. First of all, we are speaking about public measures. Secondly, the definition is based on a number of contingencies which may lead to reduction or loss of income. These contingencies include old age, invalidity, death of income earner, sickness, maternity, employment injury and unemployment. The definition also includes the provision of medical care and benefits for families with children.

Social Security in the Organised Sector

Social security is the responsibility of both the Central and the State Government. The Constitution of India provides that the state shall, within the limits of economic capacity make effective provision for securing public assistance in case of old age, sickness, disablement, unemployment and other cases of adversities. It was realized that the government cannot remain a silent spectator with regard to protection of workers against various risk. The government has, therefore, framed schemes to provide social security benefits for the workers in the organized sector. The schemes have been designed in the same pattern as those existing in the developed countries.

The schemes available in India for the workers in the organized sector are given in Table 1.

Table 1: Social Security Schemes for Organised Sector

Type of benefit	*Government/Quasi Government*	*Industrial worker in organized sector*
1. Old age	Pension, Contributory Provident Fund, Gratuity	Employers Provident Fund (E.P.F.), Gratuity
2. Survivor benefit	Family Pension Lumpsum Payment	Deposit linked Insurance Scheme
3. Unemployment	Does not arise	Retrenchment benefit
4. Employment injury /invalidity	Ex-gratia relief	Workmen's Compensation Act
5. Medical care	Treatment in Govt. hospital/Reimbursement	Employment State Insurance Scheme (ESI) other benefits
6. Sickness	Medical leave at full pay	Sickness leave under ESI Scheme

7. Maternity Benefit	Maternity leave	Maternity benefits under Maternity Act

Promotion and Protection. The objective of the social security schemes that have been extended to the workers in the organized sector is to "protect" the workers against certain risks to which they are exposed because of uncertainties. Such schemes can be categorized as protective measures. Protective measures seek to provide guarantees or enforceable entitlement to those affected by specific contingencies by compensating them for the loss of income or additional expenses arising thereby.

There is considerable unemployment and under-employment prevalent in the rural sector. Faced with massive and persistent poverty and a large unorganised working population in the rural and urban areas, the development schemes for the unorganized poor have aimed at averting or ameliorating conditions or contingencies such as low income, unemployment, sickness and disability. Direct anti-poverty programme in India comprises a wide range of programmes: (a) Improvement of agricultural income through irrigation, credit facility, technical assistance ad subsidies, (b) Employment generation such as Jawahar Rozgar Yojana, (c) Asset endowment (example; Land Reforms, IRDP), (d) Backward area development programme, (education) Provision for basic need such as housing, slum improvement, primary education, health (f) The public distribution system.

These schemes aim at "promoting" the living conditions of the people and can be categorized as "promotional measures". Promotional measures have so far constituted the main approach in regard to the unorganized poor. The dominant reliance in India on promotional measures, with virtual neglect of protective measures is due to fiscal and administrative constraint.

While getting benefits of the promotional measures some people living below the poverty line may cross the line, at the same time in he absence of suitable protective measures, some families above the line will also go below the poverty line because of uncertainties like death, sickness, disability of the earning members of the families.

It is now being realized the "promotional" measures alone cannot be successful in reducing poverty in India. Along with "promotional" measures appropriate protective measures are also necessary to save them from the worst form of deprivation. "Promotion" and "protection" do not represent an either or dichotomy and in fact have a complementary role.

Socials Security in the Unorganised Sector

The organized sector of the economy is relatively small comprising about 10 per cent of the workforce, almost the entire rural sector is unorganized. About 90 per cent of our workforce are in the informal sector, majority of whom are in rural areas. About 75 per cent of total population live in rural areas and 30 per cent of population live below the poverty line. Of the total population, 40 per cent are workers and 26 per cent of total main workers are agricultural labours. Of the total females there are about 26 per cent workers and about 16 child labour per thousand persons. About 4 per cent of total workers are above 65 years of age and 2 per cent are disabled, which includes 0.2 per cent totally disabled.

The workers in the unorganized sector practically have no social protection. The massive poverty in our country is partly due to low wages and partly due to lack of secure employment throughout the year. The employment generation schemes cannot deal with the problems of low wages in the unorganised sector specially when there is larger scale unemployment. The Minimum Wages Act, 1948 is the major legislation concerning the unorganized workers. The Act seeks to protect real wage of the worker and provides for fixation of minimum wage for scheduled employments. Once the minimum wage is fixed for any particular employment the employer cannot pay a worker wage less than the minimum wage.

We have seen four decades of development planning. The progress made in translating the ideas and objectives of social security enshrined in the Constitution, has been constrained by financial and other considerations. The social security expenditure accounts for only 2.4 per cent of Gross Domestic Produce (GDP). Even in Latin American countries it is around 6-7 per cent. In centrally planned it ranges between 13-19 per cent. It is around 25-30 per cent in Sweden, Netherlands, France, Belgium and Denmark. In other developed countries social security for a sizeable proportion of GDP.

Low proportion of social security is only one aspect, but the most important is its coverage. Most of the social security benefits in our country basically cater to the needs of the organized urban workforce, who constitute only one-tenth of the total workforce. There is hardly any popular social security scheme for the unorganized workers. The schemes mentioned above have poor coverage and the benefits are very little.

The National Commission on Rural Labour set up by the Government of India recommended that the following social security benefits should be provided as a matter of high priority.

a) Old age pension

b) Life insurance

c) Maternity benefit

d) Disability benefit

e) Minimum health care and sickness benefit

The Commission also recommended a comprehensive Group Insurance Scheme.

The quantum of benefits, legibility, nature and extent of risk covered under social security schemes vary from country to country. In majority of countries there are two approaches–Social Assistance and Social Insurance. Social assistance represents unilateral obligation of the community towards it's dependent groups. The social assistance programmes provide some benefits to the targeted group of people and are financed from general revenue of the state. All the states in our country have introduced old age pension scheme. The schemes usually provide for pensions to the destitute aged 60 and above with in income and no relatives bound by custom to support them.

Table 2: Social Assistance Scheme

Implementing Agency	*Scheme*	*Benefit*	*Eligibility*
1. Department of Social Welfare	Old age pension scheme	Rs. 100 per month	Persons of 60 years and above (55 yrs. In case of physically handicapped) with no source of income and residing in the state for more than 10 yrs.
2. Development of Social Welfare	Widow Pension	Rs. 100 per month	Widow having no income and none to support. Residing in the state for ten years.
3. Development of Social Welfare	Disability Pension	Rs. 100 per month	Physically handicapped and disabled persons who have been declared un-rehabilitable, whose income is less than Rs. 50 and residing in the state for at least 10 years
[illegible] Employment (West Bengal)	Unemployment Assistance Scheme	Rs. 50 per month for a period of two years	Registered unemployed with low family income and registered for two years

* Besides this there are Pension Schemes for particular type of workers.

Several Group Insurance Scheme for members of the weaker and vulnerable sections of the society have been introduced by the Central Government for implementation through the Life Insurance Corporation of India (LIC), and the General Insurance Corporation and it's subsidiaries.

Table 3: Social Security Schemes for unorganized sector and without premium by beneficiaries

Scheme	*Implemented by*	*Scale of assistance*	*Eligibility*
1. For Landless Agr. Worker	LIC and Govt.	Death of head of family Rs. 200	Age 18-60 years
2. Insurance for IRDP beneficiaries	LIC and DRDA	For natural death Rs. 3,000 if due to accident double.	For five years from commencement of cover.
3. Insurance of beedi workers	LIC and Beedi Work. Welf. Board	For natural death Rs. 3,000 if due to accident double	Age 18-60, death of head of family
4. Personal Accident Schemes	GIC or its subsidiaries	For natural death Rs. 3,000 if due to specific accident	Death of head of family, age 18-60 years Poor family
5. Hut insurance Scheme	GIC or its subsidiaries	Rs. 1000 for hut and Rs. 500 for belongings	Destroyed by fire, for poor family
6. Policy for IRDP animals	GIC or its subsidiary and DRDA	Price fixed by purchase committee insured	IRDP beneficiary

* The subsidies GIC are National, New India, Oriental, United India Insurance Companies.

Table 4

Insurance Schemes with Premium

Scheme	*Implemented by*	*Premium*	*Benefit*	*Eligibility*
1. For weaker section (23 employment)	LIC	Rs. 25 per annum (50% of premium) by member/ other organization	Rs. 5000 for natural death and double if due to accident	Age group 18-60 yrs.

2. (a) Janata Personal Accident Insurance	GIC or its subsidiary	Rs. 15 per annum	Rs. 25000 for death/perm. Disablement 50% for loss of an eye/limb	Issued in group age 10-70 years
3. Cattle and poor, Livestock Insurance	GIC or its subsidiary	4.5% of the value of the cattle	Rs. 10000 and 50% for same as 2(a)	For rural same as 2(a)
4. Pumpset Insurance	GIC or its subsidiary	Depending on pumpset	Market value of Pumpset	Agriculture pumpset
5. Crop insurance	GIC or its subsidiary	1-2% of sum insured	Insured sum damaged due to calamity	Loan from bank

* There are many schemes implemented by GIC and its subsidiaries.

The discussion will remain incomplete if we do not discuss about the schemes for payment of compensation to motor vehicle accident victims. These social security schemes are applicable to all categories of people irrespective of their income. A list of schemes for compensation for motor vehicle accident is given in Table 5.

Table 5

Compensation for Motor Vehicle Accident Victim

Scheme	*Benefit*	*Remarks*
1. Hit and run motor accident, U/S 161 of M.V. Act, 1988	Rs. 8500 in case of death and Rs. 2000 for serious hurt	Application to be made to SDO
2.Accident in case of fault	Rs. 25000 for death Rs. 12, 500 per permanent disablement	Application to Claim Tribunal (Addl. DJ in Dist).
3. Accident in case of fault	Compensation considering age, education, skill, earning etc,	Application to be submitted to Claim Tribunal

4. Motor Vehicle Accident Benefit Scheme	Rs. 2000 for death Rs.800 for permanent disablement	Application to be submitted to local P.S.

Under the Motor Vehicle Act compensations are paid to the victims or their families. These schemes are also well known, the only problem is that of complicated procedure involved which delays the payments. It is more difficult when the beneficiaries are poor from rural area, majority of whom are illiterate and have no ability to pursue their case.

Let us now discuss about the schemes without premium i.e. no premium is paid by the insured person. In such cases the premium is paid by the government or by any other organization. To the workers the schemes appear as social assistance schemes. Two such major schemes are the insurance scheme for landless agricultural workers and schemes for beedi workers. Separate notes on the schemes are given in the Annexure 1 and 2. These report are based on the data collected from the districts and other sources.

Out of 42 lakh beedi workers in our country, 26 lakh have been issued identify cards and 10.5 lakh lives are covered. The number of claims settled during 95-95 is only 11 per cent of the estimated number. Out of the 34 lakh paid by the Beedi Welfare Commissioner only 22 per cent has been utilized to disburse benefits to the families of the insured persons. Thus direct payment will cost him only 22 per cent of the total premium paid. The complicated procedure involved has deprived many eligible families. Application are also not received from all eligible families, which means there is not much awareness amongst the beedi workers.

Though the insurance scheme for landless agricultural workers are expected to benefit a large number of families, the performance appears to be far form satisfactory. A close look at the progressing different districts will reveal that no uniform pattern has been developed. The scheme is yet to have the desired coverage. Here also, the reason is the complicated procedure involve, which requires interactions at different levels and of different organizations. It is probable better to run the scheme as social assistance scheme with advance allotment of found at district level, so that immediate payments can be made.

The insurance schemes with premium are yet to make a good start. The concepts of insurance are yet to be clearly understood by the workers. It takes time to accept why the premium paid is not refundable if a worker has not suffered any crises. The workers with wage less than minimum wage, who are targeted group under the scheme find it difficult to pay the premium money, when they are unable to meet their daily needs.

It appears from the insurance scheme for the beedi workers that the total amount of claim disbursed is much lower than the total amount of premium paid. The complicated procedure involved has restricted the submission on of application and disbursement of claims. Thus without proper delivery system, in case of schemes with premium the total disbursement will be less than the total premium money received. This shows that there is still scope to reduce the premium amount. The procedure requires simplification to reach the target group.

The New Schemes

The Government of India has proposed new social security schemes for the unorganized sector in the budget proposal 1995. A National Social Assistance Scheme has been proposed to cover the poor and the needy. One component of the Scheme is to provide old age pension of Rs. 75 per month to the people above 65 years of age who are below poverty line.

A secured component provides lumpsum survivor benefits to the poor households, on the death of the primary bread earner of Rs. 5000.

The third component is the provision of sustenance for pre-national and postnatal maternity care to women belonging to poor households for the first two births. The schemes mentioned above are to be funded, jointly by the Centre and the States though Panchayati Raj Institutions.

There is also proposal for a new Group Life Insurance Scheme of the LIC, which will be implemented by the panchayats in the rural areas. Under the scheme, life cover or Rs. 5000 will be provided for a modest annual premium of Rs. 70. For poor households the beneficiary has to contribute 50 per cent of the premium, the balance 50 per cent will be equally shared and paid by the Central and State Governments. The details of the schemes mentioned above are yet to be worked out.

By getting benefits of promotional measures some people may improve their levels of living, at the same time, because of uncertainties like death, sickness, disability of the earning members, the living conditions of some people will come down. Thus, while some families may up above poverty line, simultaneously some families living above poverty line may go down below poverty line.

The New Concept

The traditional concept of social security has been developed by a historical process in relations to the conditions prevailing in the highly developed countries, with large scale industrialization and near full employment. The needs of such people are different from those in the developing countries. A person who is already employed is concerned with the protection of his income. On the other hand, a person who has no employment is primarily concerned with securing work and earning some livelihood. The traditional concept of social security, therefore, may not be adequate for application to the developing countries.

Millions in developing countries sufferer from severe and chronic deprivation. This is compounded by general uncertainty in life. Short-term, often acute, downward fluctuation in living standards are superimposed upon long-term, persistent deprivation associated with low standard of living. This is in contrast to the situation is most of the developed countries, where deprivation and adversity are less prevalent and implications are less severe. In a developed country, unfavourable outcome in economic activity may mean real hardship but in a poor country they often lead to death or destitution. Burges and Stern defined the term social security as: "Being the prevention by social means of very low standards of living irrespective of whether these are results of chronic deprivation or temporary adversity. The term social security may then be viewed as a measure of success in meeting this objective". This definition takes into account both the promotional measures and protective measures mentioned earlier. A definition in this direction is now being more and more accepted in different as far as the definition of the term social security for developing countries.

2

Construction Industry as an Informal Sector

1. Introduction

The importance of construction industry in economic development has been often overlooked, but it should be recognized as a potentially useful instrument for achieving various development goals. Several studies using the cross-sectional data have attempted to establish a quantitative relationship between construction output and economic development. Any attempt to further study the above mentioned relationship amounts to testing the constancy of the relationships already observed in the earlier studies. However, these studies have not touched upon the relationship between employment in the construction industry and economic development. The need for focusing on employment aspect is particularly great when one is concerned with the economic development of labour surplus developing countries. There is also a need to concentrate on the developing countries.

There is also a need to concentrate on the development experience of relatively large countries because the experience of such countries will be of replicable value to large countries like India. One would be interested in understanding whether employment, even if less productive, increases with development in these countries. The present study analyses the extent of employment besides the output of the construction industry. Data for the study are drawn mainly from Year Book of National Accounts Statistics, International Labour Statistics and Year Book of Construction Statistics.

The history of construction industry can be traced back to the times when man gave up Cave dwellings and started building a shelter for him. Thereafter, this industry played a vital role in the material progress of the world. Its progress is, generally, taken as an index of social and economic development of a country. It is a productive activity as it results in creation of assets. These assets will b further used for productive purposes. Therefore construction should e regarded as a 'Mother of productive activity'. Its development is interlinked with that of most of the other sectors in economy.

There is general agreement on the economic importance of the construction industry in all countries, whatever their level of economic development and the central role the industry might play in long term social and economic development. The volume of construction output, accounting for more than half the total capital formation in most industrialized and developing countries is in itself proof of the central place of the industry in economic growth and underlines the need for improving its efficiency.

In 1970s most of the developed countries employed nearly six to 10 per cent of the labour force in the construction industry. If employment in the building materials industry is also taken into account, it appears that in most countries 10 to 15 per cent of the total labour force is closely connected with the activities of the construction industry. The ILO studies have shown that, as a rule, the occupational group comprising craftsmen, production process workers and labourers, which accounts for only 30 to 40 per cent of the total labour force, accounts for 75 to 80 per cent of the construction labour force.

In terms of production, the value added in construction as a percentage of the Gross Domestic Product varies from country to country. It has been found by Turin that the percentage of value added in construction increases as the per capita GDP increases. The percentage value added in construction is high in the countries with high per capita GDP and low in countries with low per capita GDP. In countries with per capita GDP of less than $ 300 the average value added of construction is four per cent, while it is over six per cent in countries with per capita GDP greater than $ 2000. In between however, the average value added seems to be between five, and five and a half per cent. This suggests that the construction industry is set for a take-off when per capita GDP of a country crosses $ 300 mark.

2. Objectives, Methodology and Limitations of the Study

The Main objectives of the study's are:

1. To analyze the significance and growth of

construction industry in terms employment created and output generated in the industry, and

2. To examine the inter-relationship between economic development and urbanization on one hand and the significance of construction industry on the other.

The objectives are sought to be achieved by using cross-section data of different countries. While selecting the countries included in this study, Countries (only non-communist) with less than one crore population have been omitted, because large countries like India will have much to learn from the development experience of relatively large countries. The study in general is based on cross-section data with special focus on the year 1981. Related studies in this area conducted earlier were concerned only with years prior to 1981.

There are certain limitations relating to the data used in the study. No doubt international organizations have attempted to bring consistency into the definition and presentation of national accounts statistics, but many divergences from the standardized international system are still apparent in the data reported by individual countries. The industry in particular suffers from various problems which are peculiar to it and inherent in its very nature. One of these is that its boundaries are not easily definable, with the result that the industry does not form a clearly and readily identifiable economic sector. Many of the conclusions about the construction industry that are drawn in this study need therefore to be interpreted carefully. These are at best indicative only of broad trends and of orders of magnitude.

3. A Statistical Profile of the Construction Industry

A Employment in Construction Industry:

> The construction sector's manpower requirements are divers and extensive. However, one of the important features of this industry is the degree to which the industry provides employment for the semiskilled and unskilled labour. Here employment data of construction industry pertaining to 1980 or thereabouts for 27 countries are related to such variables as total population, total working population and total non-agricultural workers. Relevant data are presented in Table.

The percentage of construction workers to total population varies from 0.43 in India to 4.39 in Japan. The variation between countries is wider when male workers are considered-the ratio varies from 0.92 in India to 10.69 in Yugoslavia.

A more appropriate measure to gauge the significance of construction activity is the percentage of construction workers to total workers. This ratio too varies widely between 1.50 in India and 17.30 in Algeria.

Yet another indicator of the significance of the construction activity is the ratio of construction workers to total non-agricultural workers. This ratio for all workers varies between 3.03 in Bangladesh and 24.89 in Algeria. For males the ratio varies between 3.90 in Bangladesh and 27.16 in Algeria. Thus it could be observed that there are large inter-country variations in the significance of the construction industry.

B. Output in Construction Industry

Apart from employment in construction industry, one may also examine the output in construction industry to understand the significance of this sector. Three indicators viz., per capita value added in construction, value added in construction per person employed in construction, and value added in construction as a percentage of GOP are considered to examine this aspect. The relevant data are presented in Table 2 and 3and these figures relate to around the year 1980.

Taking per capita value added in construction (Table 2, col 4) it may be observed that it varies from $7 in Philippines to $ 1,062 in Canada. The figure for India is very low at $ 11. With regard to the value added in construction per person employed in construction (Table 2, col. 5) it varies from $ 1,424 in Algeria to $ 54,565 in the U.S.A. A third variable reflecting the share of construction output in the gross domestic product also fluctuates widely between 15.29 percent in Algeria and 2.83 per cent in South Africa.

Table 2 also provides data on variables such as per capita gross domestic product (Col. 2) and per capita gross domestic investment (Col. 3). These variables may be used to study the significance of the construction sector in economic development. In other words, it is possible to examine as to what happens to the construction sector as a country progresses. Another variable which is considered important for the present purpose is the level of urbanization (Col. 6). This variable is introduced because of its likely effect on construction industry. As the pace of urbanization increases, it makes heavier demands on housing and infrastructure which consequently enhances the demand for construction industry.

C. Significance of Construction Sector Relative to Other Sectors

What is the significance of construction sector relative to other sectors of the economy such as agriculture and manufacturing? In order to reflect upon the relative importance of the construction industry three ratios, viz., (1) agricultural output's share in gross domestic product, (2) construction output's share in gross domestic product, and (3) manufacturing output's share in gross domestic product have been considered. The data are presented in columns 2, 3 and 4 of Table 3. The data suggests that the contribution of manufacturing sector to national product is the highest among the three sectors in all countries, except Yugoslavia and Nigeria.

However, a careful observation of the data presented in column 2 of Table 3 shows, that thee are seven countries (out of 27) where the construction sector contributes more to GDP than the agricultural sector. Though the construction sector fails to assume the dominant position its contribution to output is substantial. This sector's contribution to GDP varies between 2.83 in South Africa to 15.29 in Algeria. This sector's importance will truly get reflected when one looks a the significance of construction in Gross Fixed Çapital Formation (GFCF). A substantial proportion of new investment is made in this sector as reflected in the data provided in column 7 of Table 3. Construction's share in GFCF varies from 46 per cent in South Africa to 67 per cent in Canada. That the residential buildings (an important component of the construction sector's output) occupy an important place in GFCF can be seen from column 8 of Table 3. This ratio varies widely from 12 in Venezuela and Pakistan to 44 in Egypt.

D. Growth Rates of Output in Different Sectors

The compound growth rates of output in different sectors of the economy at constant and current prices for different countries for the period 1970-85 or thereabouts are computed and are presented in Table 4 and 5. They indicate the differential growth of these sectors during the period under consideration. The data presented in Table 4 indicates that construction sector has been experiencing negative growth rates in many countries. Ten out of 27 countries had negative growth rates. The countries experiencing negative rate of growth in agriculture and manufacturing sectors are but few.

A further point that needs to be mentioned is that the growth rates of construction output vary very widely. It could be observed that Venezuela experienced a negative growth of the magnitude of-6.37, while Algeria had a positive growth rate of 17.72. While noting that the growth rates, to some extent, very depending upon the initial conditions obtaining in the country in question and the period chosen to calculate growth rates, it is still relevant to look upon the large inter-country variations in the growth rates of the construction output as those reflecting upon the nature of the construction sector. The agricultural sector and the manufacturing sector or even the gross domestic product do not seem to fluctuate as widely as the construction output. The conclusion that the construction sector's output fluctuates widely is also by and large true even when the growth rates, calculated at current prices are examined. Thus it could be noted that the construction output tend to fluctuate very widely compared to output in other sector's of the economy.

4. Relationship between Construction Industry and Development: A cross Section Study

This section mainly focuses on the relationship between employment and output on one hand development of the economy on the other. The process of development, in general, is expected to increase the pace of industrialization which, in turn, leads to more construction activity. Further it increases the levels of living of the people. Given high degree of industrialization and high levels of living of the people the demand for housing and other infrastructural facilities increases. Such increased demand is likely to result in an increase in construction employment and output. While this relationship between economic development (indicated by per capita gross domestic product) and construction activity may indeed exist, the strength of the relationship needs to be examined. In this section an attempt is made to test the relationship employing the following regression model:

Where, 'b1' is the regression coefficient corresponding to 'x1' which is defined as per capita gross domestic product in the year 1981 in US $. The relevant data are already presented country-wise in Table 2. 'a' is the constant. The dependent variable 'Y' is defined in alternative ways. As shown in Table-6 variable Y pertaining to employment is defined in nine alternative ways the adoption of alternative definitions is expected to help in identifying the strength of the relationship between the dependent variable and the exokabatory variable. All the data on which the regression model is based correspond to years around 1980.

The main objective in employing the regression model is to test the hypothesis that development has a positive effect on the employment and output generated in the construction industry. The linear regression coefficients of the above model presented in Table 6 are of help to make a judgment on the above hypothesis. Item-1 in the Table shows that the regression coefficient is significant at one percent level when the employment in the construction is defined as 'percentage of construction workers to total population'. But when the dependent variable is defined as the 'percentage of construction workers to total non-agricultural workers', the regression coefficients are not statistically significant however, the results of the regression exercise clearly bring out the positive and significant relationship between construction employment and economic development when the male work force is considered. Items 4 and 5 listed in Table 6, clearly show this relationship. Whatever be the definition of male construction employment, the regression coefficient turns out to be positive and significant. In the case of female construction employment also the regression coefficient turns out to be significant. Other definitions of female employment are not significantly related to development.

To test the relationship between output generated in the construction industry and development, Y is defined in three alternative ways (item 10, 11 and 12 of the Table – 6). The regression results show that there is a positive and significant (at one per cent level) relationship between construction output and development when variable Y is defined as (i) 'value added in construction per person employed in construction and as (ii) per capita construction output (items 11 and 12). But when Y is defined as 'value added in construction as a percentage of GDP' it is not found to be statistically significant (see item 10). A long-linear form of the above regression model (see Table 7) is employed to further examine the earlier results obtained using the linear form of the regression model. It is observed that construction employment of the economy. Construction output also has a positive relationship with the level of development of the economy when it is defined as 'value added in construction per person employed in construction' and as 'per capita construction output'.

The above results are obtained based on the data relating to 21 countries with population exceeding one crore. The countries included in the sample comprises of high developed as well as underdeveloped countries. It may not be very proper to club together the countries at two extreme stages of development in trying to understand the relationship between economic development and construction employment and output. To overcome this methodological difficulty and to distinguish between the developed and developing countries, a different regression model of the following type is employed:

$$Y=a+b1x1+b2D$$

Where b2 is the coefficient corresponding to the dummy variable D. the variable d takes values 1 or 0 depending on whether the observation in question is a developed or a developing country. All those countries with a per capita GDP of $ 1700 and above are considered as developed.

If b2 coefficient is significant it means that the observed relationship between construction and per capita gross domestic product is different between the developed and the developing countries. The result of the regression exercises are presented in Table 8. the results show that the coefficient of the dummy variable b2 is statistically significant in four of the nine cases when construction employment is considered as the dependent variable. Thus there is considerable evidence to show that there are significant differences between developed and developing countries in respect of the relationship between employment and GDP. However the dummy variable is not found to be significant when the construction output is considered as the dependent variable.

3

Informal Sector—Earnings and Mobility Pattern amongst Urban Labour

Out of the major areas of research in the urban labour market in the last decade has been the informal sector. Thought, the theoretical basis of the informal sector concept can be traced in the models of dualism, as an objective of developmental policy and also as and area for indepth empirical research, it has recently gained acceptance only. Hence, in this chapter, an attempt is made to review the literature on various aspects of the informal sector. Issues covered are: *(a)* origin of the concept of informal sector, *(b)* a review of the studies on structure of sectoral earning, *(c)* access and mobility in formal sector, and *(d)* the role of informal sector in urban economy.

Origin of the Concept of Informal Sector

Prior to the advent of informal sector concept, various classifications, such as, "organized and unorganized", "modern and traditional", "Capitalist and subsistence sector" have been used for analyzing the dichotomous nature of an urban economy. All these dualistic frames laid emphasis on the dis-continuities in the urban economic organization. They also analysed the distinguishing characteristics of these two sectors often highlighting the policies for the growth of the first sector neglecting the other. But is often argued that division of urban economy into two parts is arbitrary as the economic organization is a continuum of production activities. In fact, the unorganized enterprises may be in the process of transition and with the passing of time, they would graduate to the other sector and thus any lead to the disappearance of discontinuities. There are also other, who argued that the two-way classification of the urban economy is inadequate as the informal sector itself could be broken into two sub-sectors: *(i)* an irregular sector, and *(ii)* the informal sector proper. Despite this, the dualist frame is claimed to be more useful in the anjalysis of a urban economy.

Different labels have been used by different economists to depict the two-sub-systems of production. According to McGee, most cities of the third world can be seen as "Con-sisting of two Juxtaposed Systems of Production—one derived from capitalist forms of production, the other from the peasant system of production." Cliford Geertz preferred to decribe the two systems respectively as the "firm-centered economy" and the "Bazaar-type economy". They have also been referred to as "Upper" and "Lower" circuits of the urban economy. While these labels emphasis distinctive "organization" of production activities, another study using "modern traditional" dichotomy refers to "technology" used. Subsequently, several new labels have come into use in analyzing the dichotomous nature of the urban economy in terms of structure of employment and income. Considering the growing imbalance in urban economy, a study focused on Africa has observed that a substantial part of the growing urban population and labour force is being absorbed not in the 'enumerated' sector consisting of well-organised enterprises, but in the 'unenumerated' sector consisting of small-scale self-employed activities. Structural imbalance is also interpreted in terms of 'rich' and 'poor' sectors, where the former relies on imported capital, skill and technology and is alien to traditional societies. This corresponds to the modern-traditional sector dichotomy, which is objected on the ground that "the use of traditional" as a term of disparagement is the product of a alien culture that sees 'tradition' as being detrimental to development rather than as an integral part of a nation's culture and identity.

To this array of labels, "formal-informal sector" dichotomy has been added as a meaningful and convenient method of analysis of urban economic structure. The formal-informal sector dichotomy was first used by Keith Hart (1971) in his empirical study of Urban Ghana. One significant respect in which this study differs from those cited earlier is that it highlighted the existence of a variety of new income-generating activities in trade and service categories in an urban economy. The study also observed that most of these activities are concentrated in the "unorganise" sector and as they are not covered by the existing data collecting machinery, they fall into the "unremunerated" sector. The workers engaged in them mainly worked as self employed, as against the wage labourers in the "enumerated" sector due to the inadequate opportunities in the formal sector on the one hand and lack of skills and experience on the part of the new entrants (or migrants) on the other. In the study, the terms—informal income generating activities, unorganized sector, unenumerated sector self-employed individual, urban proletariat and individuals earning less than the legal minimum wage-are used more or less alternately and interchangeably to represent the 'informal sector'. This study, not only, described the informal sector but also as highly unproductive and consisting of surplus labour.

Recognizing the fact that it takes a long time for the fruits of general development policies to percolate down to the poorest sections of the population, the Employment Mission Report on Kenya of the ILO has introduced this term in its report. With this adoption by IOL, this concept stated gaining considerable importance in the literature on development policy in general and employment policy in particular. The report also stressed that in order to promote employment opportunities and to achieve more equitable income distribution, it is important to concentrate development efforts on a specific target group, i.e., the informal sector.

Subsequently, under the auspices of ILO's World Employment Programme, a number of country studies (Kenya, Columbia, Sri Lanka and Philippines) and city studies (ILO, 1970, 1971, 1972, 1974, 1976a) Joshi, et al., (1980) Lubel, (1974) Sethuraman (1976a) were carried out. The main achievement of these studies is the shift in the emphasis from a development strategy based mainly on economic growth (wherein employment was treated as residual) to the strategy which focused employment as prime objective.

Structure of the Informal Sector

Despite its wide usage, the informal sector concept "has remained somewhat obscure and even caused confusion in some quarters". Sethuraman opines that "the informal sector, as its name suggest, is not formal in its character. However, there are a number of characteristic features of the informal sector, either derived on apriority basis or from several empirical studies on urban areas in developing countries. The two sectors are mainly distinguished in terms of mode of production, oranisation and scale of operation. According to the ILO Employment Mission Report on Kenya, the informal sector has the following characteristics: easy entry for the new enterprises, reliance on indigenous resources, family ownership of enterprises, small – scale operation, labour-intensive and adopted technology, informally acquired skills of workers and unregualated and competitive markets. Correspondingly, formal sector enterprises possess characteristics obverse to the above. The report considered the enterprises but not the individuals in the formal and informal classification.

The report also distinguished the formal and informal sectors in terms of government fovours. The formal sector activities are officially reconginsed and fostered by the government by providing direct accesses to credit, foreign exchange concession, etc. On the other hand, informal sector activities are "largly ignored, rarely supported, often regulated and sometimes actively discouraged by the government. In terms of income, the report characterizes the informal sector-either agricultural or non-agricultural, with low incomes resulting in primacy of risk and uncertaintly.

Sethuraman observes that the report included mainly squatter settlement enterprises as belonging to informal sector at one point, while at other all enterprises not recognized by the government are included. Moreover, the characteristics proposed are particularly appropriate to Kenya and may be less relevant to general case.

To avoid ambiguity while distinguishing the informal sector from formal one, economist attempted to provide an analytical base. According to John Weeks, the distinction is based on "the organisational characteristic of exchange relationships and the position of economic activities vis-à-vis the state. The nature of exchange relationship is primarily a consequence of the economic insecurity of operation in the informal sector, which in turn, is a direct consequence of the latter's limited access to the resources of all types." Basically, the formal sector includes government activity and private enterprises, which are officially recognized, fostered, nurtured and regulated by the state. On the other hand, operations in the informal sector do not carry these benefits, they are outside the system of official regulations and benefits, have no access to the formal credit and foreign technology. Further, in contrast to the formal sector, the informal sector due to its product and factor markets, is charactersied by small-scale operations, labour intensive techniques, low income levels and indigeneous ownership.

Heather and Vijiay Joshi have distinguished, organhised and unorganized sectors in Bombay under three major heads market structure, technology and relationship with government. While doing so they highlighted Weeks' analysis of the two sectors. They defined informal sector as "those engaged in economic activity, who are not identifiably performing it for the formal sector. Illustrating the Indian situation, Papola opines that the distinction between the formal and informal sector employment can be made on the basis of registration of the manufacturing enterprise under the Factories Act. Under the Act registration is obligatory, once the employment size of the enterprise reaches 10 workers with the use of power and 20 workers without the use of power. Once the enterprise is a registered factory, the conditions of work, such as recruitment, working conditions, hours of work, leave, payment of wages, dismissals, etc., get regulated. In the case of non-factory organization the conditions of work are into regulated and are quite informal.

Dipak Mazumdar's study describes informal sector as the "unprotected" sector. He observes that employment in the formal sector is protected by the actions of trade unions and government, while the same is denied to the informal sector labour. Mazumber has brought out the distinction more sharply by arguing that entry into the informal labour market is unrestricted, whereas in the formal sector labour market it is restricted by artificially raised hiring standards, norms and procedures.

Keith Hart, who gave initial currency to the concept of informal sector, distinguished formal from informal income opportunities, the latter encompassing all non-wage sources of income, whether legitimate or illegitimate. This distinction is essentially based on wage earning and self-employment.

Kenneth King defines informal sector as follows: "their informality derives from their being unrecognized in government employment statistics ad operating in the main out of makeshift shelters on urban waste lands, road sides and forest fringes.

In his study on Calcutta, Harold Lubell commented that the informal sector constitutes the residual labour market of the last resort, which persons enter as self-employed, low-income producers of marginal goods and services for lack of any other means of earning a livelihood. It is also identified as a reservoir of traditional and modern skills, which can be made productive if effective demand is created for them.

While attempting to quantify informal sector. Souza and Tokman stated that this sector "comprises of all those engaged in domestic service, casual labour, the self-employed and employees of white collar, blue collar ad family workers in enterprises with a total staff of not more than four persons".

Breman, considering mode of production as a basis for analytical distinction between formal and informal sectors, describes the latter as containing a "mass of the working poor, whose productivity is much lower than it is in the modern urban sector from which most of these people are excluded. To him the distinction refers to two economic sectors, each having its own structural consistency and dynamics.

Focusing on the employment and development policies in an urban economy, Sethuraman defines informal sector as one which, "consists of small-scale unites engaged in the production and distribution of goods and services with the primary objective of generating employment and income to their participants notwithstanding the constraints on capital—both physical and human—and knowhow.

From the above description of informal sector it is clear that it is an all-inclusive term. Generally this sector includes into only traditional artisans, services and petty traders but also small units in manufacturing, construction, trade and commerce, transport and service sectors engaged in the production of goods and services (with sole proprietorship or engaging more persons) which operate on very small scale and have no formal business organization.

Thus, the various elements of the definition of the informal sector indicate a broad spectrum of heterogeneous of urban poor households, ranging form employment in small-scale industries to self-employment, skilled and unskilled, including street vendors and petty traders with low and irregular income. This heterogeneity of informal sector led to the search for a common criterion for the identification of informal sector enterprises. As the informal sector provides employment primarily to urban poor any attempt to promote employment and raise their income should identify the characteristics, problems and constraints of enterprise rather than of individuals. Thus, the focus of enquiry should be primarily on the enterprise rather than on the individual participant in the informal sector.

Attempts in this regard evolved a set of characteristics in identifying informal sector enterprises. They are: it should employ 10 or less than 10 persons, it operates on an illegal basis; contrary to government regulations, members of the household of the head of the enterprise work in it. It does not observe fixed hours/day of operation. It operates in a semi-permanent or temporary premises or in a shifting location. It does not use any electricity in the production process. It does not have access to formal credit. Its output is normally distributed to the final consumer and workers engaged in it should have less than six years of formal schooling. The informal sector thus includes all enterprises with ten person less engaged in manufacturing, trade and service sectors.

To suggest a possible criterion to delineate between formal and informal sectors, Mazumdar states that formal sector is identified with unionism, government regulation, enforced welfare and wage legislation of so-called 'enumerated' establishments. He also pointed out that sometimes it is difficult to arrive at a cut-off point between these sectors in terms of size of employment. Finally, he feels that "our judgement should be the ultimate criterion in most situation". However, most of the studies on urban labour markets adopted size of employment as the criterion for the informal sector enterprises. (In some cases some operational and diagnostic criterion are also used).

Significance of the Informal Sector

The series of city studies conducted at the instance of ILO's World Employment Programme reveal that the share of urban labour force engaged in the informal sector ranges anyshere from 20 to 70 per cent in the urban areas of many developing countries (see Appendix Table 3.1) the magnitude of employment in this sector is estimated to be around 60-70 per cent in Nairobi and Kamasi 53-38 per cent in Bagota 50 per cent in Jakarta ad Lagos 45 per cent in Calcutta,

Bombay, and Ahmedabad and 30 per cent in Abid Jan.

In India several studies have attempted to identify the informal sector for a city as a whole and estimated the proportion of work force in this sector.

Based on the establishments data of the Directorate of Employment, Bombay with correction for 1961, Joshi and Joshi have estimated the size of the urban informal sector for greater Bombay at 47.7 per cent and 49.5 per cent for the years 1961 and 1971 respectively. They have considered employment in the unorganized sector as residual of organized sector which includes all public and private sector establishments with more than 25 employees.

Using the same criterion and data source, Deshpande has arrived at two different estimates of the size of the informal sector in Greater Bombay. Without correction for 1961, and 51.3 per cent in 1971. With correction for 1961 as well as for 1971, he estimated the same to be 39.5 per cent and 42.0 per cent for the respective periods.

Based on the census data, Bose has estimated informal sector employment for Calcutta city to be 28.3 per cent. He has included all non-registered manufacturing units employing less than 20 persons and all non-manufacturing units employing four or less than four workers including independent works.

Mazumdar has estimated the size of informal sector employment in Delhi to be 61.4 per cent and 53.8 per cent in 1961 and 1971 respectively. He has followed that size of employment criterion, i.e., residual workers in all units employing 10 or more workers, while using the employment 10 or more workers, while using the employment statistics pubished by the Directorate of Employment, Delhi.

Another study by (Operation Research Group) on Madras Metropolitan Area has found out the share of employment in the informal sector to be 50 to 70 per cent. This study also used the size of employment of the enterprise as the criterion in estimating the informal sector. All workers employed in the establishments with 10 or less including unattached workers are included in the informal sector.

Jan Breman in his empirical study on Valsad town in south Gujarat has focused on the size of the informal sector. According to the study, around 75 per cent of the work force is found to be existing in the formal sector.

Some studies even showed that the share of employment in informal sector has been increasing over a period of time. Papola in his study on Ahmedabad has pointed out that the share in informal sector employment has increased from 40 percent in 1961 to 47 per cent by 1971. The study also shows the extent of informal sector in different activities: in agriculture and allied activities it constitutes 50 per cent, in trade and commerce 67 per cent, in transport and communication 76 per cent and in other services 49.5 per cent.

Similarly Mazumdar's study on Delhi has observed that the share of employment ir, informal sector in urban Delhi has marginally increased from 61.36 per cent in 1960 to 62.97 per cent by 1980.

Further, based on the census establishment data of 1971, Viswakarama has observed that the size of informal sector employment in India is around 76 per cent. Thus, on the whole, it appears that the size of the informal sector in terms of employment ranges from a minimum of 45 per cent to a maximum of 75 per cent in India.

In terms of income generation, the informal sector also contributes substantially to the urban regional income. In Asuncion (Paraguay), San Salvadoe (El Salvador) and Lima (Peru) it was estimated to be 33, 25 and 30 per cent respectively.

In Ahmedabad (India) the contribution of the sector to the total domestic product of the city was around 28 per cent. From this it is evident that the urban informal sector has been playing a major role in absorbing labour and in generating incomes for the poor.

Structure and Determination of Earnings

Labour earnings in the informal sector are relatively very low compared to their counterparts in the formal sector. They are almost half or even less compared to the formal sector wages. But they are found to be still higher than what the migrants from rural areas earn at the place of their orgin. Merrick found formal sector wages to be more that 85 per cent higher that informal sector earnings in Belo Horizonts, Brazil even after the effects of experience and education were allowed for.

According to Mazumdar, much of earning diferential between formal and informal sector can be explained by the age, sex, and educational characteristics of workers in the two sectors. He observed that informal sector workers in Brazil appear to be concentrated at either end of the age distribution span, have less education on averages and are more likely to be female than formal sector workers. It is also pointed out that in addition to differences of personal characteristics, there are structural factors, which contribute to these income disparities. (The income inequality among households and population in rural and urban areas of selected developing countries are presented in Appendix Table 3.2).

Several attempts were male to empirically identity and measure the impact of these factors on earnings in the urban areas. Deshpande in his study on Bombay analysed the average earnings in terms of skill and sector. The study traced out significant variations in earnings in terms of skill and sector. The study traced out significant variations in earning between skilled and unskilled workers as well as among casual, small establishment and factor workers. In his study he points out that the earnings of the skilled workers in all sectors of work are more than those of semi-skilled workers and almost double the earnings of unskilled workers.

Earning differentials are also related to type of employment and castes, Radhakrishna et. al., in their study of Ahmedabad observed that average earnings of factor workers are higher than the average earnings of office establishment workers, self-employed workers and casual workers. Significant variations in earnings are also observed between Harijans and Adivasis for the same type of work in the informal sector.

Patel, in his study on Ahmedabad, also concluded that average earnings of organized sector workers are higher than those of self-employed and casual workers in the informal sector. Study also observed that significant differences in the average earnings between organized and unorganized sector workers.

Earnings in the informal sector are also found to be varying according to the status of the workers. Subrahmanyam et al., in their study on construction workers in Ahmedabad have noted that significant variations in earnings are existing between causal and regular workers in the construction activity. Besides this, the study also observed that the percentage of distribution of casual workers in the lower earning group (Rs. 61.90) is nearly 60 per cent compared to the percentage of (25 per cent) regular workers in the same earning group. On the other hand, in the highest earning group (Rs. 251+) only 2 per cent of casual workers are traced compared to 13 per cent of regular workers.

Papola and Subrahmanyam in their study have observe earning differentials among three different types of workers, viz., establishment workers, independent workers and casual workers.

Average earnings of establishment workers are substantially higher compared to the earnings of casual workers. Independent workers earnings are even twice the earnings of casual workers. His study also shows that the percentage distribution of workers in the lower earning class is more in the casual workers and insignificant (only 1 per cent) in the higher earning class. On the other hand, establishment workers and independent workers are concentrated in the higher earning group.

Organisation Research Group's study on the slums of Madras Metropolitan area analysed the variations in earnings in terms of employment status, skill levels and activity type. The study observed that informal worker (including self employed) are earning low monthly incomes compared to the organized sector employees. Further their proportion in the lower earning group is around 70 per cent while the same is around 4 per cent in the higher earning group. By contrast the proportion of organized workers in the lower earning class in 21 per cent while the same is around 57 per cent in the higher income class.

Thus evidence shows that the earnings in the informal sector are very much low compared to the formal sector. Further, the earning differential among different sectors and among different activities in the informal sector itself appear to be significantly influenced both by the personal characteristics of workers and by the structural factors in the urban economy. In addition to these factors, persistent wage differences between formal and informal sectors have also been explained both in terms of rational behaviour of formal sector firms and in terms of wage legislation and power unions.

Access and Mobility in the Informal Sector

Studies referred to so far are unanimous about the point that informal sector absorbs the urban poor because of its unlimited capacity to expand, low capital intensity and lack of entry restrictions. Therefore, the growth of informal sector leads to achieve more equitable distributions of employment opportunities and incomes in the urban areas. However, Breman warns such type of description of the informal sector as a "dangerous and misplaced romanticism of the hard fight for existence at the bottom of the urban economy". He states that jobs in the informal sector are scarce and entry is not that free as assumed by many. Even the lowest incomeyielding activities in the informal sector are controlled by groups of people on the basis of social and communal bonds, Papola also states that in a large number of trades carried out in the informal sector, "the social and communal connection and financial resources are necessary to buy entry" It is thus concluded that the labour market is not just dualistic but it is highly fragmented on particularistic basis and rooted in primordial conditions in an urban economy. Radhakrishna et al., in their study also found that social background influences to a larger extent the employment in the informal sector. Further Breman even observes that education, which is a force to achieve greater equality of opportunities has in fact led to greater inequality in access to jobs.

Scarcity of employment opportunities also affects labour mobility. Even the naïve assumption of Todaro that the unskilled workers who migrate to towns drift into urban traditional sector and subsequently graduate to the modern sector later, seems to be unrealistic. This is due to the persistence of low earnings (flat wage earnings) at the point of entry. Low wages discourages attachment of workers to an individual firm and instability prevents acquisition of skill and perpetuates low wages. As a consequence, those who join the lower ranks of the urban labour system usually remain there. Though horizontal mobility is limited between sectors, occupational mobility within the sector is not altogethers negated. Empirical evidence suggests that intra-sectoral mobility in the informal sector is quite encouraging. In a study on Jakarta it is observed that only two-thirds of the migrant workers remained in the job of their first entry while one-third of migrant workers have moved to higher earning jobs in the informal sector after learning new techniques and skills. Mobility from low earning jobs to higher earning jobs among different activities in the sector and between the sectors is argued to be primarily influenced by the life time aspirations of the informal sector family to get the children upto the social scale, i.e., to higher wage and salary employment in the formal sector. However, Mazumdar points out that the probability of getting a formal sector job is greater in the case of open unemployed "regulars" compared to that of "visitors" who scratch at this and scratch at that in the informal sector for a temporary period of time. Another study shows that workers sometimes prefer to accept lower average earnings in the informal sector for a change to profit from the opportunity for rapid upward mobility in the informal sector as formal sector has little flexibility in terms of conditions of work and promotion.

Role of Informal Sector Sector in Urban Economy

In view of its labour absorption and income generation capacity, the role of informal sector in an urban economy needs no emphasis. As such, the informal sector is accorded a crucial place in the process of development. However, development of the informal sector with a view to increasing employment and productivity levels raises a number of issues. According to Breman, there are basically two approaches in this regard. To one school of through the informal sector is an inevitable but transitory phase in the development process as a 'buffer zone' providing some income and employment to the urbon poor for their sustenance till the formal sector is able to absorb them. Another approach, encouraged by ILO and World Bank, views the informal sector as the most promising source of development. It also emphasizes the need to develop it to have strong linkages with the formal sector on the basis of mutual advantage in place of exploitative relationship that presumably exists. However, Breman expresses no definite preference to either. He is skeptical about the end result as the background interests of policy executing elites always rest with the development of the formal sector. Papola and others suggest that in order to promote informal sector, the supportive programmes should aim at technological upgrading and enhancement of scale of informal production units which inevitably lead to its transformation and submersion into the formal sector.

Despite this controversy regarding its ole in the development process, informal sector is considered to be the source of future growth and hence, an integral part of urban employment strategy. Guy Standing argued for a strategy for expanding the informal sector as a means of combating urban unemployment and related reemployment problems. Finally, Sethuraman argues that the informal sector has a due role to play in the process of urban development.

For promoting the informal sector as a source of future growth several arguments were put forth. It was argued that besides creating employment to the unskilled labour force in the developing countries that informal sector plays an important role in formation of human capital by providing access to training at a substantially lower cost when compared with the formal sector training institutions. It was also held that informal sector not only relies heavily on the use of local resources but also plays a significant role in recuperating and recycling of the waste material in the urban areas. Finally it was argued that development of informal sector through economic planning automatically ensures equitable distribution of development benefits to the hitherto neglected section of the society. Thus, in all respects informal sector is poised as the most promising sector in the development process.

Conclusion

On the basis of the above discussion it can be concluded that informal sector has been playing a major role in absorbing labour and in generating incomes for the urban poor. On the whole, it appears that the size of the informal sector in terms of employment ranges between 45 per cent and 75 per cent, while its contribution to the urban regional income is around 30 per cent. However, earnings in the informal sector are much lower that earnings in formal sector. It can also be concluded that within the informal sector itself there are significant differences in earnings among different activities. Earnings are determined by the personal characteristics on the one hand and institutional characteristics on the other. While the inter-sectoral mobility is taking place on a lesser note, the intra-sectoral mobility especially in the informal sector is much restricted and less common due to social, communal and financial restraints. However, the very existence of the informal sector helps to some extent in achieving equality in the distribution of income and also in providing gainful employment to the urban poor. Hence, the development of he informal sector should form part of the urban development strategy.

STRUCTURE OF PAYMENTS AND MEASUREMENT OF EARNINGS

In terms of mode of payment and the nature of average earnings, different sectors of our study exhibit varied patterns among the heterogeneous groups of labour force. The method of payment ranged from daily wage rate of contract wage rate of a construction labourer to a completely formalized system of monthly payment of salaries with additional perks for an employee in a large establishment. These differences in the method of payment give rise to several problems of measurement of average earnings of the workers. It is attempted to solve these problems in the following way:

Self-Employed: The self-employed in our study are mainly drawn from craft-based manufacturing and repair, personal services and those engaged in petty trade. These include, Technicians, Tailors, Milk-producers, Hoteliers, petty Traders, Auto-Rickshaw Drivers, Dobhies, etc. As most of them did not engage any hired labour, the value added could be equated with the averages earnings. To estimate their average earnings, we have elicited information relating to their earnings in the previous month, days worked, additional income from any other source, such as rents etc.

Casual Workers: The casual and unattached workers are drawn mainly from construction activities and rickshaw pullers. The construction workers are generally dependent on labour contractors for employment. The average wage they received showed little variation amongst the workers, probably because of identity of skills. However, there were variations in the number of days of work availability, mainly because of differences in skill levels. After arriving at number of days worked in an year, their monthly earnings are computed with the help of daily wage rate.

Casual workers included in the services sector were mostly rickshaw pullers. Their earnings are largely in the form of piece rate. Their monthly earnings depend on the number of days worked. In respect of those who operate with rented rickshaws, the number of days for which the rickshaw is available, also influences their monthly earnings. Among other factors which will have a bearing on the earnings of worker operates are important. In the case of these workers, average monthly earnings are computed, taking into account the number of days worked and average daily earnings.

Domestic Servants: Workers in this sector, mainly females, take to this activity to augment the household earnings. They are generally paid on monthly basis. Their earnings also include payments in kind. The imputed value of these payments, in kind also, is taken into account while arriving at their monthly average earrings.

Informal Establishment Workers: The main activity groups to which the selected sample households belong, are machine using and repair, poultry, tailoring, whole-sale and retails shops, hotels and restaurants and bankers. The systems of payment prevalent in this sector are: (1) monthly or fortnightly payment and (2) piece rate payment. In the case of those who receive wages on monthly or fortnightly basis, average monthly earnings are worked out taking into account their actual earnings. In the case of those, who are paid on 'piece rate' basis, the number of days worked, the amount of work put in per day during the working days and the rate of payment are considered while calculating the monthly average earnings.

Formal Sector Workers: Sample workers included in this category belong to activities such as machine using and repair, tailoring, poultry, whole-sale and retail shops, big hotels and restaurants. Usually those who are retail shops, big hotels and restaurants. Usually those who are engaged in these activities are paid on monthly basis. The system of fortnightly payment also is prevalent in some quarters. Their actual earnings and perks, if any, formed the basis for calculating average monthly earnings. Income accruing from sources other than wage, such as, rents, etc., are also taken into account.

Table 1: Estimated Share of Urban Labour Force in the Informal Sector in Selected Developing Countries

Area	*Year*	*Percent*
Africa		
Abidjan (Ivory Coast	1970	31
Lagos (Nigeria)	1976	50
Kumasi (Ghana)	1974	60/70
Nairobi (Kenya)	1972	44

Urban Areas (Senegal)	1976	50
Urban Areas (Tunisia)	1977	34
Asia		
Calcutta (India)	1971	40/50
Ahmedabad (India)	1971	47
Jakarta (Indonesia)	1976	45
Colombo (Srilanka)	1971	19
Urban Areas in West Malaysia (Malaysia)	1970	35
Singapore	1970	23
Urban Areas (Thailand)	1976	26
Urban Areas (Pakistan)	1972	69
Latin America		
Cordoba (Argentina)	1976	38
Sao Paulo (Brazil)	1976	43
Urban Areas (Brazil)	1970	30
Rio de Janerio (Brazil)	1972	24
Belo Horizonte (Brazil)	1972	31
Urban Areas (Chile	1968	39
Bogota (Colombia)	1970	43
Santo Domingo (Dominican Republic)	1973	50
Guaya Quil (Ecuador)	1970	48
Quito (Ecuador)	1970	48
San Salvador (El Salvador)	1974	41
Federal District and State of Mexico	1970	27
Mexico D.F., Gaudalajara and Monterey	1970	42
Asuncion (Ponaguay)	1973	57
Urban Areas (Peru)	1970	60
Urban Areas (Venezuela)	1974	44

Concas (Venezuela)	1974	40
Kingston (Jamaica)	1974	33

Source:

1. PREALC : Sector Informal, p. 30.
2. Kalmann Schaefer: Sao Paulo: Urban Development Employment (Gevena, ILO, 1976), p.67.
3. H. Joshi, H. Lubell and J. M only: Abidjan: Urban Development and Employment in lvory Coast (Geneva, ILO, 1976), p. 54.
4. Mara Institute: *The Informal Sector of Colombo* (Srilanka), (Colombo, K.O. 1978), p. 26.
5. Donald See and A.G. Ottman: "The Urban Informal Sector: A Glimpse of the Malaysia Experience" in ASEAN, *Seminar on Informal Sector,* Jakarta, 11-16 December 1978.
6. Chia Lin Sien and Chia Siow Yue: "The Informal Sector in Singapore", *ibid.*
7. M. Irfan: "The Informal Sector in Pakistan" (Unpublished Manuscript), p. 3.
8. M.P. Van Dikj: Development du sectum non-structure an Senegal: the etude development son context et son potential, JASPA (Dakar, ILO, 1977), p. 1.
9. Biplab Dasgupta: "Calcutta's Informal Sector" in Bulletin (Institute of Development Stadies, University of Sussex), October 1973, p. 67.
10. S. Tambunlertchai et. al.: "The Urban Informal Sector in Thailand", *ibid.*
11. PREALC: Guidelines for action in the informal secor of Central Kingston, PREALC working paper, No. 101, Santiago, ILO 1976), p. 6.
12. Mahonmad Driva: Le Secteem non-structure dans l' economic Tunesienne d' après le recensement des establishments, paper presented at the Seminar: Labourers Petite Production Marchand en milieu urban, africain, organized by IEDES, Paris, March 1979.
13. Victor Tokman: Technologia Pena el Sector Informal Urbano, PREALC: Documento Occasional No. 4, Jan., 1978, Table 1.

Notes and References

1. Louis Emmerij, "A New look some strategies for Increasing Productive Employment in Africa", *International Labour Review,* Sept. 197, pp. 202-204.
2. Guy Standing, "A Trichotomous Model of Urban Labour Markets", in Urban Labour Markets", in *Urban Labour Market Behavioru in Developing Countries,* (ed,) by Subbaiah Kannappan, International Institute of Labour Studies, Geneva, 1977.
3. T.G. McGee, "Peasant in the Cities: A Paradox, a Paradox, and most Ingenious Paradox", *Human Organisation* (Washington), Summer, 1973, p. 138.
4. Clifford Geertz, Peddlers, Princes: Social Change and Economic Modernization in two Indonesian Towns, University of Chicago Press, Chicago, 1963, Chapter 3.
5. Milton Santos, *The Shared Space-The Two Circuits of Urban Economy and their spatial Repurcussions,* London, Methuen, 1975.
6. Lloyd G. Reynolds, "Economic Development with Surplus Labour: Some complications", in *Oxford Economic Papers.* (New Series), March, 1969.
7. S.V. sethuraman, "The Urban Informal Sector: Concept Measurement and Policy", *International Labour Review,* July-August, 1976, p. 70.
8. John Weeks, "An Exploration into the Nature of the Problem of Urban Imbalance in Africa", in *Manpower and Unemployment Research in Africa,* Montreal, November 1973, pp. 9-36.

9. Louis Emmeriji, *op. cit.*, p. 202.
10. Hart Keith, "Informal Income Opportunities and Urban Employment in Ghana", in Journal of Modern African Studies, London, March, 1973, pp. 61-89. An earlier version of this article was presented to the conference in Urban Unemployment in Africa held at the Institute of Development Studies, University of Sussex, in September 1971.
11. International Labour Organization, Employment, Incomes, and Equality: A Strategy for Increasing Productive Employmetn in Kenya, (Geneva, 1972).
12. S.V. Sethuraman, *op. cit.*, p. 13.
13. __ __ "The Informal Sector in Developing Countries: Some Policy Implications", *Social Action,* July-Sept., 1977, p. 196.
14. International Labour Organization, *op. cit.*
15. *Ibid.*
16. S.V. Sethuraman, *op. cit.*, p. 72.
17. John Weeks, "Policies for Expanding Employment in the Informal Urban Sector for Developing Economies", *International Labour Review,* Vol. III, No. 1, Jan. 1975, pp. 2-3.
18. __ __, *op. cit.*, p. 4.
19. Heather and Vijay Joshi, *Surplus Labour and City: A Study in Bombay,* Bombay 1976.
20. __ __, "The Informal Urban Economy and the Boundaries", *Economic and Political Weekly,* Vol. 29, March, 1980.
21. T.S. Papola, *Urban Informal Sector in a Developing Economy,* Vikas Publishing House, Pvt. Ltd., New Delhi, 1981.

22. D. Mazumdar, The Urban Informal Sector, World Ban Staff Working Paper No. 211, Washington, 1975, p.1.

23. __, "Labour Supply in Early Industrialisation — The Case of Bombay Textile Industry", *Economic History Review,* August 1973.

24. Hart Heith, *op. cit.,* p. 73.

25. K. King, "Kenya's Informal Machine Markers: A Study of Small Scale Industry in Kenya's Emergent Artisan Society", *World Development,* April-May, 1974.

26. Harold Lubell, "Under Development and Employment in Calcutta", *International Labour Review,* Vol. 109, No. 1, July, 1973, p. 28.

27. P.R. Souza and V.E. Tokman, "The Informal Sector in Latin America", *International Labour Review,* Vol. 114, No. 3, Nov. – Dec., 1976, p. 356.

28. Jan Breman, "A Dualistic Labour System: A Critique of the 'Informal Sector' Concept" in *Economic and Political Weekly,* 27 November, 1976, p. 1871.

29. S.V. Sethuraman, *The Urban Informal Sector in Developing Countries: Employment, Poverty and Environment,* ILO, Geneva, 1981.

30. International Labour Organisation, World Employment Programme, Geneva, 1978, p. 13.

4

Employment Potentialities in Informal Sector

Even after four decades of planned development, agriculture continues to be the mainstay of population in India and about 65 percent of the work force depends on the agricultural sector. Agricultural labourers constitutes the largest chunk of the labour force. Most of the agricultural labourers are illiterate, unskilled and hail from depressed communities. Most of the agricultural laboureres are landless and purely depend on wage paid employment in agriculture. Agricultural employment is seasonal and intermittent in character. Agricultural labourers are very often the victims of seasonal unemployment and in the years of severe drought, the problem is more acute. Their wages are low which permits them hardly to have hand to mouth existence. During the lean periods, they have to depend on cultivators and unscrupulous money lenders who often exploit them. Thus most of the agricultural labourers have become indebted.

The employment in agriculture depends upon a

host of factors like size of land holdings, irrigation, soils, cropping pattern, climatic factors, supply of labour, intensity of cropping, etc., of which irrigation is the primary factor of production. Inspite of the huge investments made to develop irrigation in the Five Year Plans, still about 70 percent of the net area sown is under rainfed conditions where crop harvest is uncertain due to failure or uneven spread of monsoons.

The wages of agriculture labourers are low and inexorable economic necessity compels them to work for even low wages. The low incomes enable them to have a low standard of living which ultimately results in low labour productivity in agriculture. There is little uniformity with regard to agricultural wages and method of payment from state to state and from region to region. There are wage differentials between men and women and between different occupations. Very often women labourers are paid less than male labourers. The working conditions of agricultural labourers are miserable and they have to work from sun rise to sun set in hot or cold weather. Agricultural labourers are victims in the vicious circle of poverty, unemployment, low wages, low standard of living and indebtedness.

The data on size of land holdings in India reveal that most of the cultivators are small and marginal farmers. Their farm incomes are very often low. From generation to generation, the land holdings are further divided and fragmented due to division of land among heirs. Consequently the average size of the holdings has gradually declined. Due to low and uneconomic holdings, the small farmer has no capacity to hire labour for agricultural operations. The small farmer attempts to substitute family labour in the place of hired labour reducing the employment opportunities of landless labourers. Thus, the problem of agricultural labour is multi-dimensional and has its roots in the simple truth that they carry on their struggle for survival bare handed without being able to obtain strength and succour through any means.

The National Commission on Agriculture has rightly pointed out that the levels of living of the bulk of agricultural labourers have undergone little improvement inspite of the sincere efforts made for the removal of poverty in the Five Year Plans. More specifically, the structural measure to realign the production relations within agriculture in favour of agricultural labourers and other weaker classes and legislative support to wages in agriculture have little to show by way of concrete results. Ironically, even the spectacular upsurge in agricultural production in the regions of "green revolution" does not appear to have brought within its wake a uniform and substantial improvement in wages. Thus, neither the general economic development nor agricultural development and not even reform measures through the instrumentality of state in India seem capable of reaching far enough to purvey hope and viability to the class of people who bore the major burden of the immiserising economic transition.[1]

Based on the historical perspective. National commission on Agriculture identified major aggravating factors that are likely to worsen the problems of agricultural labourers over the coming decades. Firstly, the demographic additions to the labour force over the next about three decades are estimated to be very substantial. Secondly, the expansion of non-agricultural avenues of employment is unlikely to be fast enough to provide significant relief to agriculture from the pressure of population for many decades ahead. In fact, there is a noticeable apprehension among the students of Indian economy that the critical factor in the sustained development in future is not so much the capacity of the agricultural sector to provide increased production as its capacity to do this without throwing out surplus labour. Thirdly, in the absence of basic institutional reforms and effective controls to promote selective mechanization, technological change in agriculture can easily prove to be a bane rather than a boon to agricultural labourers[2].

It should be obvious from the above that the problems of agricultural labourers arise not so much from the specific weaknesses and deficiencies of this class as from the basic maladjustment in the total Indian economy due to lack of fast enough growth along with structural and technological changes. Hence, the principal instrument for tackling these problems is the totality of planned efforts for development[3].

As India's economic growth depends on the performance of its agriculture which in turn depends upon the economic well being of the agricultural labourers, several development programmes have been implemented to improve the economic conditions of the largest section of work force and to divert the surplus labour in agriculture to non-agricultural sectors through the process of industrialization. To access the improvements in the Grassroots Economics several enquiries have been conducted from time to time. It would, therefore be interesting to have a brief look at the results of these Enquiries on the Grassroots Economics in India.

The government of India, Ministry of Labour had so far conducted seven Agricultural/Rural Labour Enquiries. The main objective of these Enquiries is to collect information on the socio-economic characteristics of agricultural/rural labour and to study the changes in socio-economic conditions brought about by economic development programmes with a view to formulate action programmes for improving their living conditions.

The first two Agricultural Labour Enquiries were conducted in 1950-51 and 1956-57. The seven Rural Labour Enquiries for which the scope of coverage was widened to include all rural labourers (including agricultural labourers) were carried out in 1963-65, 1974-75, 1977-78, 1983, 1987-88, 1993-94 and 1997-98. The data collected during these Enquiries related to the structure to households, employment and unemployment, average daily earnings, consumption expenditure and indebtedness.

It has to be noted that the comparability of data collected during these enquiries has been affected to some extent on account of changes in the concepts and definitions adopted and the estimation procedure followed for the different Enquiries. In the First Agricultural Labour Enquiry, the agricultural labour household was defined on the basis of employment criterion while from the Second Agricultural Labour Enquiry, the basis was changed to income. While only households engaged in crop production were covered for the First Enquiry, all households engaged in activities like dairy farming, horticulture, raising of livestock, etc., were also included in the Second Enquiry. The concepts and definitions adopted for the First and Second Rural Labour Enquiries were identical. From the Third Rural Labour Enquiries onwards, rural and agricultural labour households have been classified on the basis on the activity status and employment as recommended by the Committee of Experts on Unemployment Estimates (1970).

Growth of Agricultural Labour Households

According to Agricultural and Rural Labour Enquiries, the number of rural households was estimated at 58.9 million in 1950-51, 100.5 million in 1983 and 119.5 million in 1993-94. The number of rural households has increased by 102.9 percent in 1993-94 over 1950-51. The rural labour households are estimated to have increased from 17.9 million in 1977-78 to 45.8 million in 1993-94. The agricultural labour households have increased from 17.9 million households in 1950-51 to 36.2 million in 1993-94 registering an increase of 102.2 percent. The percentage of agricultural labour households to rural households was worked out to 30.4 percent in 1950-51, 30.7 percent in 1983 and 30.3 percent in 1993-94. It is interesting to note that 86 percent of the rural labour households were estimated to be agricultural labour households in 1964-65 while it has remained at 79.0 percent in 1993-94. The data in the table prove that more than 80 percent of the rural labour households have agricultural labour as the main source of livelihood. According to the Rural labour Enquiry, 1993-94, 55.95 percent of the agricultural labour households have no land of their own and the remaining 44.05 percent possess some land.

Methodology

Agricultural labourers constitute the largest chunk of rural work force. Agriculture continues to be the largest sector in Indian economy and its economic development depends no less on the performance of its agricultural sector. The performance of Indian agriculture depends mostly on rainfall since irrigation facilities are available only for one-fourth of the gross cropped area. Due to rapid growth of population and slow growth of non-agricultural labour population without land base depending on wage paid employment in agriculture for their livelihood. Agricultural labourers form the most unorganized and neglected section of the rural society who are the victims of the low wages, seasonal unemployment, low incomes, poverty and indebtedness. Their meagre incomes hardly permit them to meet both the ends. To ameliorate the conditions of these vulnerable sections, several developmental programmes have been implemented to relieve them from the clutches or poverty and indebtedness. Inspite of four decades of planned development it is still believed that their conditions have not improved. How far it is true? Hence, in this study an attempt has been made to enquire into the Grassroots Economics. This micro level study will be highly useful to understand the economic conditions of this major section in-depth.

Objectives of the Study

The study is based on the following objectives:

1. To study the social conditions and asset values among the agricultural labourers.
2. To study the pattern of employment of

agricultural labourers and to identify the factors influencing the employment of agriculture in the study area.

3. To study the wages of agricultural labourers and to identify the factors influencing the agricultural wages in the study area.
4. To analyse the income and expenditure patterns of agricultural labour households.
5. To estimate the savings, indebtedness and poverty among the agricultural labourers.

Sampling Design

The sample households for the study have been selected using three-stage random sampling method. The study is confined to Chittor district. All the mandals in the district have been considered for the selection of first stage units of sampling. For the selection of mandals , all the mandals in the district were grouped into three categories, viz., developed, developing and less developed on the basis of selected economic indicators like:

1. Percentage of agricultural labourers to main workers;
2. Percentage of net area sown to total geographical area;
3. Percentage of net irrigated area to net area sown;
4. Percentage of land holdings of below one hectare to total holdings;
5. Percentage of Scheduled Caste and Scheduled Tribe population to total population. From each category, one mandal was selected using ransom

sampling method. Thus, the study covered three mandals in the district. Accordingly, Erpedu mandal in the developed, Gudipala mandal in the developing and Gangavaram mandal in the less developed categories are selected.

All the villages in the selected mandals have been considered for the selection of second stage units. For the selection of villages, all the villages in the sample mandal have been grouped into five categories on the basis of percentage of agricultural labourers to main workers. One village was selected from each group using random sampling method.

From each sample mandal, 80 sample agricultural labour households have been selected in probability proportion to existing households under each category and in each selected village. Thus, the study covered 240 sample agricultural labour households. The list of selected sample agricultural labour households in each mandal is given.

Distribution of Sample Agricultural Labour Households in the Selected Mandals

Sl. Category	*Erpedu*	*Gudipala*	*Gangavaram*	*Total*	*Percentage to total*
1. Landless Households	34	30	27	91	37.92
2. Households with Land (in acres)					
(a) 0-1	14	28	11	53	22.08
(b) 1-2	5	14	17	46	19.17
(c) 2& Above	17	8	25	50	20.83
Total	80	80	80	240	100.00

Out of the total 240 sample households, 91 households are (37.92 percent) landless and labour households who possess lands constitute 149 (62.08 percent). Among the sample households with land 53 households possess less then 1 acre (22.08 percent) 46 households possess between 1 and 2 acres (19.17 percent) and 50 households possess above 2 acres (20.83 percent) The above table reveals that majority of agricultural labour households are either landless or possess small holdings.

Agricultural labour household has been defined for the study on the basis of income criteria. An agricultural labour household is one which derives more than 50 percent of the annual family income in the form of wages earned through hiring out labour of the members of the family in the preceding year of enquiry.

Study Design

The main focus of the study is to examine the wages, employment, income, expenditure and indebtedness of the agricultural labourers in Chittoor district so as to ascertain the Grassroots Economics. The study also makes an attempt to estimate the poverty among the agricultural labour households and to identify the factors influencing the employment and wages in the study area. The study has the agricultural year 1988-89 as the reference year.

Collection and Analysis of Data

The survey method was used to collect the required data for the study. The required information and data were collected on various aspects form the sample respondents through personal interview with the concerned with the aid of schedules conducting a pilot survey. Some minor changes were incorporated in the schedule after completing the pilot survey. Due care was taken to have cross checks in schedules of the level of knowledge of the respondent and all the precautions were taken to ensure the accuracy and reliability of data. All the schedules have been scrutinized so as to appraise the qualitative and quantitative aspects of the data before each schedule was passed for tabulation.

REFERENCES

1. Government of India, "Report of the National Commission on Agriculture, 1976, Part-XV, Agrarian Reforms", Ministry of Agriculture and Irrigation, New Delhi.
2. Government of India, "Seventh Five Year Plan," 19850-90, Volume II, Planning Commission, New Delhi, 1985.
3. Sen, Amartya, *Poverty and Famine: An Essay on Entitlement and Deprivation*, Oxford Publishers, Oxford, 1980.

5

Agricultural Labourers as an Informal Group

Concepts

The definitions adopted for various concepts used in the study are furnished as given:

Agricultural Labourer

Agricultural labourers are those persons who are employed on another person's land to perform various tasks in connection with planting, preparation of the soil, ploughing, sowing weeding, harvesting, etc. Thus, all those labourers who work for wages whether in kind or cash or in both in agricultural operations are considered as agricultural labourers.

Casual Labourer

Agricultural labourers who have not been in continuous employment and are not working for a single landlord all the days regularly on the day preceding to this enquiry are considered as casual labourers.

Attached Labourer

Agricultural labourers who have been in continuous employment under some contract or on some particular understanding during the major part of the year preceding the date of enquiry are considered as attached labourers.

Agricultural Labour Household

A household which derived more than 50 percent of the total annual income from wage employment in the preceding year is considered as agricultural labour household.

Contract Labour

Contract labour are those labourers who combine into a group to enter into an agreement with the landlord to perform a type of work and share the remuneration received from the landlord as per the agreement arrived at by them before entering into the concerned work.

Employed Person

Any person who performs some work for remuneration or profit during the period of enquiry is to be considered to be an employed person. Persons who are working on some job but temporarily absent during the course of enquiry due to illness or injury or leave or due to temporary suspension of work on account of bad weather, etc., also come under employed persons.

Persons of the age of 14 years and above during the period of enquiry, if found assisting the operations on farm and working for at least 1/3 of the normal working day though unpaid on account of being a member of the family of the cultivators will be treated as employed.

Wages

Wages mean cash or kind received as remuneration for any work done or services rendered during the period of enquiry. They may be in cash or in kind or in both.

Perquisites

Certain allowances which are given as a matter of routine out of custom to the workers in addition to the wages paid, whether the wages are paid in cash or in kind or in both are known as perquisites. They include many things like clothes, vegetables, tobacco, tea, pan, grain, etc. All such allowances also include things which are given to the workers as consideration for past or present services.

Unemployment

All persons above the age of 14 years during the period of enquiry, who are not doing any work or job, and are seeking a work or job for remuneration or profit, are considered to be in a state of unemployment.

Hours of Work

Hours of work constitute the normal working hours for specific agricultural operations fixed according to the tradition in the area concerned.

Household Income

Household income constitutes the earnings of all

the earners and earning dependents who are the members of the household in addition to the share of the income of the family accruing from property, cultivation of land, livestock, home grown products, etc.

Consumption Expenditure

It consists of expenditure on non-durable and durable consumption items, services (education, health care, convenience and entertainment) and marriages and other social ceremonies. The wages received in kind by the casual and permanent agricultural labourers are included in the total consumption of the households for estimating household consumption.

V. Sundara Rajan's[4] paper concluded that the landless agricultural labourers mostly due to lack of adequate opportunities of non-agricultural employment do not obtain regular employment all the year round. On an average, a male agricultural labourer was employed for 141.2 days of which agricultural work alone provided employment for 112 days while the female labourer was employed for 73.2 days of which agricultural work accounted for 68 days. The author concluded that the solution to the problem of unemployment lies not only in speeding up of land reforms and reorganization but in accelerating industrial development.

V. Sreenivasa Rao's[5] study made an attempt to study the employment and net income of agricultural labourers in Madras State and the results reveal that on an average the agricultural labourer is found to have worked for a period of $6^{1/2}$ months in a year. Adult females work for a period of four months because of their involvement in household duties. Non-agricultural work forms a very small proportion of the total employment of agricultural labourers. Child agricultural labourers are also employed for as much as nine months.

Shah and Singh[6] studied the impact of green revolution on rural employment in North-West Uttar Pradesh. The authors have concluded that green revolution has a positive impact on rural employment in general and negative impact on employment due to tractorization.

Nirmal Kant Saha's[7] paper concluded that due to irrigation facilities, the intensity of cropping has increased. With assured irrigation the cultivators are able to produce double and multiple crops. This cropping; intensity ultimately increases the employment potential. Now-a-days in the irrigated villages the agricultural labourers are getting more work as compared to those in unirrigated villages. As a result, they are also less unemployed per month.

Singh, M.L.[8] conducted a study in 1970-71 in two villages (Burdiha and Ramideva) of Palamau district of Bihar with the objective of estimating the degree of unemployment/under-employment of labour in the rural areas and identifying the factors influencing labour utilization. The author observed that the main problem of rural unemployment is one of under-employment rather than of open unemployment of workers. The nature of agricultural production is such that it provides employment on seasonal basis. There is, however, a considerable scope for increasing farm employment by increasing the irrigation facility and the extent of area under HYV programme. It has been suggested that redistribution of land would raise the farm employment.

Grewal and Kahlon[9] conducted a study in 1969-1970 in the central plains and South-Western districts of the State of Punjab to examine whether farm mechanization displace human labour or not. They have established that mechanization generates off-farm employment by raising demand for mechanical inputs.

Singh *et al.*,[10] conducted study in 1971-72 to examine the effect of new agricultural production technology on farm labour in different categories of farms. They also examined the effect of farm mechanization

on labour employment in different agricultural operations in different categories of farms. The extent of seasonal variations was another aspect of the study. The pattern of labour use in different months indicated that the variability in labour employment decreased as the level of adoption of modern technology gave more employment to farm labour. But the level of mechanization which, in fact, is closely related to HYV technology did not give any evidence of reduction in labour use.

Garg *et al.*,[11] studied the employment effect of high yielding varieties. It was observed that high yielding varieties of paddy, maize and wheat enhanced the employment opportunities by 19.47, 15.31 and 19.42 percent respectively over the corresponding local varieties.

K. Singh[12] made an attempt to examine whether agricultural wage rates and employment increased, declined or remained constant in the IADP district between 1962-1963 and 1967-1968. He also tried to measure the impact of new agricultural technology on labour employment. The author concluded that the hired labour employment per hectare increased in most of the IADP districts, but in some of them, the effect of the increased employment on real wage earnings was neutralized by the decline in daily real wage rates.

S.S. Acharya's[13] study revealed that the adoption of HYV has increased human labour employment by 31.7 percent. The installation of pump sets has decreased labour use by 18 to 20.3 percent. However, mostly it is accompanied by the adoption of HYV and an increase in the intensity of cropping. Thus, the pump operated participant farms do not employ less human labour compared to the non-mechanised non-participant farms. Even after accounting for the differences in the cropping intensities, 27.6 percent decrease in labour use due to pump installation is offset by 36.3 percent increase in labour use due to the adoption of HYV and thus the net result is to increase labour demand by 8.7 percent. The introduction of tractors reduces labour employment by 50.1 percent. However, the area under the HYV to the extent of 35 percent, partially, offsets the negative effect of tractorization on employment. Tractorization enables the farmers to increase the intensity of cropping by 35.5 percent which again has a positive effect on labour employment. Thus, the net result is that, though tractorization, would have negative effect on human labour employment, the tractor operated farms employ 12.7 percent more labour compared to the non-mechanised non-participant farms.

Marothia[14] in his paper examined the impact of farm mechanization on the employment of bullock and human labour with respect to different farm sizes and the impact of farm machanisation on cropping intensity, farm production and income on tractor and bullock operated farms of different sizes. The study reveals that farm mechanization increases human labour employment and reduces the demand for bullock labour employment with the increase in size of holding. The study also concludes that farm mechanization increases cropping intensity, farm production and farm income with the increase in the size of holding.

Gangwal and Paramatma Singh[15] in their study on the impact of green revolution on the employment of agricultural labour conducted in Haryana area observed rapid increase in the use of mechanization in agriculture. Date regarding the use of agricultural labour were collected at two time periods, i.e., 1961-62 and 1971-72. The results of the study reveal that due to green revolution the employment opportunity on farms has increased and there has been a rapid growth in mechanization.

Chawla[17] made an attempt in his paper to examine the effects of green revolution on the volume of employment, wage earnings and wage rates of agricultural labourers in Amritsar district of Punjab at the three points of time, *i.e.*, 1966-67 pre-adoption period, 1970-71 and 1973-74 (post-adoption period). On different average holdings, the cropping intensity increased by 11.3 to 19.8 percent in 1970-71 over the pre-adoption year (1966-67) and further increased between 5.88 and 11.72 percent in 1973-74 over 1970-71. Due to greater cropping intensity made possible by irrigation, use of farm machinery and high-yielding varieties of crops, the overall labour requirements increased on different farm situations. Family labour got more employment on all farms, especially on the small-farms, while the increase in the employment of casual labour was more marked on the medium and large farms.

Dixit[17] conducted a case study in Rohtas district (Bihar) to examine the change in the volume and pattern of human labour employment with the adoption of high-yielding varieties of paddy. The study concludes that the adoption of HYV would improve the living conditions of the farmers by increasing their economies and would provide them more employment opportunities. Raju's[18] paper examines the effects of new farm technology on hired human labour employment in an IADP district, West Godavari. The results of the study show that wages and employment of labour have increased significantly from 1967-68 to 1970-71 and new technology has significantly contributed to this increase.

Verma's[19] article is an attempt in studying the impact of farm mechanisation on human labour use. The investigation was carried out in the Jaipur district of Rajasthan. The study reveals that mechanization of certain farm operations decreased labour requirement on small and medium size farms and large size farms too, per hectare labour input decreased by the increased cropping intensity not only compensated this decrease by increased the aggregate labour requirement. This suggests that relative approach should be adopted towards mechanization. Introduction of farm mechanization (tractors) on small and medium size farms at eh present level of crop technology would displace human labour. However, on large sized farms, mechanization (tractors) may safely be introduced without much danger of displacement of labour.

Sadhu and Singh[21] made an attempt to examine per acre requirements of labour on different categories of holdings and the share of labour in the total variable costs as a result of new agricultural strategy. The authors tested the hypothesis whether the introduction of new farm technology leads to a reduction in farm employment or not. They found that demand for labour per acre went up as a result of the adoption of new farm technology. The labour requirement in the case of HYV seeds and new farm practices in proportionately higher. Increasing cropping intensity, farm mechanization and adoption of other improved farm practices have promoted employment of farm labour.

Singh and Pandey's[22] paper shows that the new agricultural technology has not only led to an increase of the opportunity of labour employment in the agricultural sector but it has also helped in providing regular employment to the agricultural labourers.

Khatkar and Hasija[23] in their study, made an attempt to examine the labour employment pattern in relation to farm size and level of mechanization. Per hectare utilization of human labour marginally declined but the employment of hired labour even on per hectare basis was higher on machanised farms. Thus, mechanization has set the healthy trend of solving the unemployment problem of landless agricultural labourers.

C.K.Joshi and M.R.Alshi's[24] study reveal that per hectare female labour use on HYV cotton and jowar farms is more as compared to the local variety farms.

HYV cotton farms used about 157 percent more female labour per hectare over the local variety, while in the case of jowar crop, the HYV jowar used 26 percent more female labour over the local variety. The adoption of HYV of cotton and jowar increased the requirement of hired female labour to a large extent, implying thereby an increase in the employment opportunities for female labour seeking agricultural wage employment.

Vinod Kumar, et al.,[25] in their study have observed that a woman labourer is employed for 307 days on an average and the employment per woman labour was slack in August and September. The months of October to May are the peak periods for agricultural operations. During this period, harvesting of sugarcane crop, sowing the harvesting of rabi crops take place. In the months of June and July, the women labour is mostly employed in non-agricultural work. Regarding the employment pattern of women labour, a woman labourer is employed for 203 days or 66 percent in agriculture and 104 days or 34 percent in non-agricultural activities. In agriculture, female employment was the highest in harvesting, threshing and winnowing (26 percent) followed by interculture (19.9 percent, sowing (2.60 percent) and preparation of land (1.6 percent). In the study area, women workers are mostly employed on casual basis.

P.S. Grewal's[26] study highlights that among the Scheduled Castes, the female agricultural workers are employed for less number of days than that of male agricultural workers. A female worker got employment for 132 days as compared to 241 days for a male worker in a year.

Wages

Vyas's[27] study results shows that as far as the wages of agricultural labourers are concerned, the general impression of probably low wages was confirmed. It was observed that the average daily earnings for the casual male labourers, who constituted the bulk of the agricultural labour force ranged from 87 paise in Hasteda to Rs. 1.45 in Ankodia. In Afawa the average earning on the days employed was 95 paise per day and in Rampura Rs.1.18. It was observed that in all except Hasteda village payment in cash was the most important, or rather exclusive form of payment to the agricultural workers. As such as 97 percent of the total remuneration was paid in cash. But in Hasteda which was a subsistence oriented, poor village, 40 percent of the payment was made in kind. Apart from the wages, the agricultural labourers were also given perquisites during certain operations. These perquisites varied from village to village and were guided more by custom.

Sreenivasa Rao's[28] study made an attempt to study the employment, wages and income of agricultural labourers in Madras State. The author concluded that the average wage of men is higher than for women and children for all the agricultural operations. Sowing and transplanting operations in the case of men and women are much better paid than other operations. The method of wage payment was 57 percent in cash, 36 percent in kind and 7 percent in both cash and kind. Harvest operations are generally paid for in kind.

Rajendra R. Mehta's[29] study of landless labour of Botad reveals that 90 percent of the agricultural labour force were illiterate and 95 percent of the agricultural labourers lived in their own mud-huts; the remaining in rented houses. Almost all these families spent 70 percent of their income on food. Before 1951, the labourers were paid at the rate of about 35 paise for half a day and they had worked only for four hours. Since then it had increased. Since 1951 some changes had taken place in their social and economic conditions. A male labourer was paid Rs. 2.50 a day, a female labourer Rs. 1.50 and a child 75 paise. The wage also varied with the seasons.

James W. Gough's[30] paper indicates with some degree of certainty that in Punjab and Haryana, the growth rate of real agricultural wages is rising and that this rise is associated with green revolution. However, without consideration of the number of days worked, daily wages tell little about the economic situation of a group. Growth rates of production rose much more than growth rates of real wages, showing that the labourers received only a small share of the gains.

Nirmal Kant Saha's[31] paper concluded that due to irrigation facilities, the intensity of cropping has increased. With assured irrigation, the cultivators are able to produce double and or multiple crops. This cropping intensity ultimately increases the employment, this has also influenced the wage rate in agricultural practices. The labourers are also getting maximum daily wages for different operations in the irrigated villages.

Herdt R.W. and E.A. Baker[32] examined the impact of HYV on agricultural wages. The authors concluded that there is a perfectly elastic supply of labour in all regions. In most of the regions, money wages were significantly correlated with production of one or more foodgrain crops.

There is no correlation between real wages and production. There was a significant correlation between wheat production and real wages in Bihar, West Bengal and Punjab, the high yielding variety of wheat showed and high correlation with wages.

K. Singh[33] made an attempt to examine whether agricultural wage rates and employment increased, declined or remained constant in the IADP districts between 1962-63 and 1967-68. He also tried to measure the impact of new agricultural technology on labour employment. The author concluded that the daily real agricultural wage rates declined over the period 1962-63 to 1967-68 in many of the IADP districts.

Bardhan[34] has observed that any increase in irrigation and cropping intensity is likely to raise agricultural wages more in an area where there is limited supply of labour and high non-agricultural wage rates. Adoption of labour saving technology and on the other side over trade unionization may adversely contract the positive response of agricultural wage due to increase in irrigation and cropping intensities. The study revealed that irrigation and multiple cropping have a positive impact on not only wage income but also on the daily wage rates of agricultural labourers.

Pandey's[35] paper is based on an empirical analysis of demand and supply variables that influence agricultural wages in India. The author finds that labour market functions well in the contemporary setting of Indian agriculture. The demand variables are found to be much more powerful than supply variables in determining agricultural wages, the former show higher coefficients in districts where the pressure of population on cultivated land is high. The supply variables, on the other hand, are relatively more important in districts where the pressure of population on land is low. The author concluded that the real solution to the problem of low wages of agricultural labourers lies in the development of agricultural sector itself. The study also suggests that the supply of labour may not be much in excess of demand in the region of present study.

Indira Hirway's[36] study results show that, on the whole, agricultural wage rate does show a positive trend, though the rate of increase is very low. Adequate data is not available to give a full explanation about the trends in agricultural wages, but the available data suggest that irrigation and industrial development are likely to have a positive influence on the agricultural wage rate.

Rajinder Sondhi and Karam Singh's[37] study says that the average wage of agricultural labourers in Punjab increased from Rs. 2.45 in 1960-61 to Rs. 3077 in 1965-66 and to Rs. 7.21 in 1970-71. Thus, after the introduction of high yielding varieties, the wages increased by Rs. 3.44. In contrast, before the new varieties were introduced, the increase in wages was only Rs. 1.23. The wages index increased from 176 in 1966-67 to 283.35 in 1970-71, showing that the real wages index increased from 100 in 1960-61 to 152 in 1970-71. The parity of real wage index with real per capita income in Punjab fluctuated around 100 upto 1967-68, but has consistently improved to 118 in 1970-

71. This shows that the labourers' monetary position has relatively improved in Punjab.

Gangwal and Paramatma Singh[38] examined the impact of the green revolution on agricultural wage rates in Haryana State. The study revealed that there was no increase the real wages of agricultural labourers between 1961-62 and 1971-72. The increase in wages is nothing but money illusion. The wages have increased in the same proportion as the consumer price index of the agricultural labourers. On the whole, it can be concluded from this study that agricultural labour has not gained anything from the green revolution so far as the standard of living is concerned.

Grover and K.V. Rai's[39] study shows that during ten years period from 1961-62 to 1970-71 which can be termed as the period of agricultural revolution, the wages of agricultural labour remained constant in terms of wheat, gram and bajra in Haryana State. Similarly no change was observed for the wages of industrial labour during this period. Though the money wages showed considerable increase during the period under study, the inflationary trend in prices has kept the real wages at the same level, *i.e.,* as in 1961-62. Thus, the agricultural labourers were not benefited by the green revolution.

Pandey and Dixit's[40] paper attempted to study changes in labour productivity and wage rate. There was some upward shift in the productivity of labour during the periods 1954-57 and 1966-70 in Ferozepur district. During the period, wages rose by 130 percent while the consumer prices increased approximately by 93 percent. Some of the increase in wages might be attributed to the rise in the productivity.

Singh and Singh[41] conducted a study of sixteen villages in Bihar to identify the factors determining agricultural wages. They observed that the agricultural wage rates respond positively to the percentage of area irrigated, the intensity of cropping and the average size of holding, and negatively to the proportion of agricultural labour households.

Gupta[42] examined the inter-regional and inter-seasonal variations in wage rates and studied the relationship between the wage rates and the intensity of employment in different seasons. The study was conducted in Gurdaspur district in Punjab in 1972. The study observed wide variations in the overall wage rates which varied from Rs. 4.23-5.90. Whereas the agricultural wage rates varied from Rs. 4.55-6.32, the non-agricultural wage rates varied over a narrow range of Rs.3.99-5.15 in the different regions. Further, the movements in the agricultural and non-agricultural wage rates were almost coinciding. In respect of non-agricultural wage rates, no significant inter-period (or within region) variations were observed. Inter-regional non-agricultural wage rates, however, varied significantly. The study observed no significant correlation between the intensity of employment and wage rates could be established.

Chawla's[43] study revealed that the wage earnings, wage rates and employment of the casual labour have gone up since the introduction of HYV technology. The demand for permanent farm labour has gone up on all the farms. Similarly, the annual earnings of permanent farm labourers increased by 38 percent from Rs. 1,630 in 1966-67 to Rs. 2,260 in 1973-74. On the whole, it is observed that with the introduction of

HYV technology and associated modern inputs, the volume of employment, earnings and wages in the rural areas have gone up during the last eight years.

Bhuyan and Chakraverty[44] conducted a study on wages and income in rural areas of Orissa. It is observed that during the last decade, the real wage rate has remained more or less constant due to the steep rise in the cost of living index. The wage rate varies from coastal districts to other districts of the State. The variation in the wage rate depends on both the demand for and study of labour. The wage rate trend during the last decade shows that the money wage rate has increased by hundred percent whereas the ral wage rates has remained constant.

The results of the Raju's[45] study reveal that there was significant increase in both the money wages and real wages for hired labour from 1968-69 to 1970-71 in West Godavari district. The money wages have shown a much higher rate of increase than the real wages, which may be due to the rise in the cost of living of measeured by the consumer price index for agricultural labourers. In the upland areas, where there is no such green revolution, the increase in wages was less whereas in the deltaic and where there is much green revolution, the increase in wages was a substantially high. The increased demand for labour generated by the green revolution as well as the consequent rise in wage rates may continue as far harvesting operations are not mechanized.

On the basis of the 25th round of N.S.S. for 1970-71, Deepak Lal[46] concluded that in contrast with earlier studies, it is found that the real agricultural wages rose in India during the period 1956-57 to 1970-71.

However, in the first-half of this period (1956-57 to 1964-65), real wages were constant, but in the following period 1964-65 to 1970-71, they rose sufficiently to offset the earlier decline and the stagnancy or decline of real wages till 1967-68 in the green revolution belt.

On the basis of arguments given by different authors Rohini Nayyar[47] observed that real wage rates, in one of the main green revolution regions, *viz.*, Western Uttar Apradesh, showed no tendency to rise over the period 1959-1960 to 1973-1974. In fact, after 1970-1971, real wages have declined. There is no simple casual relationship between the introduction of HYV technology that leads to increased agricultural output and trends in real wages. A complex set of factors in the realm of political economy the bargaining power of the agricultural workers, the power of the land-owners, the nature of contractual relations between the two, the availability of alternative employment and the pattern of land ownership would also influence real wage rates.

REFERENCES

1. V. Sundara Rajan, "Employment and Earnings of Hired Labour in Agriculture," *Indian Journal of Agricultural Economics,* Vol. 12, No. 2, April-June, 1957.
2. V. Sreenivasa Rao, "Employment and Net Income of Agricultural Labourers in Madras", *Khadi Gramodyog,* Vol.12, No.3, December 1965.
3. S.L. Shah and L.R. Singh, "The Impact of New Agricultural Technology on Rural Employment in North-West Uttar Pradesh", *Indian Journal of Agricultural Economics,* Vol. 25, No. 3, July-September, 1970.

4. Nirmal Kant Saha, "Irrigation and Economic Change Among Agricultural Labour", *Khadi Gramodyog,* Vol. 17, No. 12, September, 1971.
5. M.L. Singh, "Unemployment in Rural Areas of Palamau District (Bihar)", *Indian Journal of Agricultural Economics,* Vol. 27, No. 4, October-December 1972.
6. S.S. Grewal and A.S. Kahlon, "Impact of Mechanisation on Farm Employment in the Punjab", *Indian Journal of Agricultural Economics,* Vol. 27, No. 4, October-December, 1972.
7. Singh, et al., "Impact of New Agricultural Technology and Mechanisation on Labour Employment", *Indian Journal of Agricultural Economics,* Vol. 27, No. 4, October-December, 1972.
8. Garg et al., "Impact of Modern Technology of Rural Unemployment", *Indian Journal of Agricultural Economics,* Vol. 27, No. 4, October-December, 1972.
9. K. Singh, "The Impact of New Agricultural Technology on Agricultural Wage Rates and Employment in IADP Districts", *Indian Journal of Agricultural Economics,* Vol. 27, No. 4, October-December, 1972.
10. S.S. Acharya, "Green Revolution and Farm Employment", *Indian Journal of Agricultural Economics,* Vol. 28, No. 3, July-September, 1973.
11. Marothia, D.K., "Impact of Farm Mechanisation on Labour Employment : A Case Study", *Khadi Gramodyog,* Vol. 20, No. 5, Fegruarhy, 1974.
12. A.C. Gangwal and Paramatma Singh, "Impact of Green Revolution on Farm labour", *Eastern Economist,* Vol. 61, No. 21, May 24, 1974.

13. Chawla, J.S., "Impact of Green Revolution on Employment, Earnings and WageRates (A Case Study in District of Amritsar)", *Indian Journal of Agricultural Economics,* Vol. 29, No.3, July-September, 1974.

14. Dixit, R.S., "Rural Employment and HYV of Paddy: A Case Study", Kurukshetra, Vol. 24, No. 5, December, 1, 1975.

15. Raju, V.T., "The Impact of New Farm Technology on Human Labour Employment", *Indian Journal of Industrial Relations,* Vol. 11, No. 4, April 1976.

16. Verma, R.C. "Tractors and Employment of Rarm Labour", *Eastern Economist,* Vol. 70, No. 26, January 30, 1978.

17. A.N. Sadhu and A. Singh, "Agricultural Growth and Farm Employment", *Indian Journal of Agricultural Economics,* Vol. 21, No. 4(1), January, 1979.

18. B.N. Singh, R.K. Pandey, "Impact of New Agricultural Technology on Labour Employment in Bihar", *Manpower Journal,* Vol.24. No.4, January-March, 1981.

19. P.K. Khatkar and R.C. Hasija, "Labour Employment Pattern in Relation to Farm Size and Level of Mechanisation in Dry Area of Mohindergarh District", *Manpower Journal,* Vol. 27, No. 3, October-December, 1981.

20. K. Joshi and M.R. Alshi, "Impact of High Yielding Varieties on Employment Potential of Female Labour : A Study in Akola District (Maharastra)", *Indian Journal of Agricultural Economics,* Vol. XL, No. 3, July-September, 1985.

21. Vinod Kumar, T.R. Singh, S.R. Yadav and R.P. Singh, "Employment and Income Pattern of Woman Labour in Modern Agriculture in District Meerut (U.P)", *Indian Journal of Agricultural Economics,* Vol. 40, No. 3, July-September, 1985.

22. P.S. Grewal, "A Study in to the Pattern of Employment and Wage Structure for Scheduled Castes Women in Punjab Agriculture : A Case Study", *Indian Journal of Agricultural Economics,* Vol. 40, No. 3, July-September, 1985.

23. V.S. Vyas, "Agricultural Labour in Four Villages-Some Observations", *Khadi Gramodyog,* Vol. 11, No. 5, February, 1965.

24. V. Sreenivasa Rao, "Employment and Net Income of Agricultural labourers in Madras", *Khadi Gramodyog,* Vol. 12, No. 3, December, 1965.

25. Rajendra R. Mehta, "The Landless Labour of Botad", *Yojana,* Vol. 23, No. 26, January 1, 1970.

26. James W. Gough, "Agricultural Wages in Punjab and Haryana", *Economic andPolitical Weekly,* Vol. 6, No. 13, March 27, 1971.

27. Nirmal Kant Saha, "Irrigation and Economic Change Among Agricultural Labour", *Khadi Gramodyog,* Vol.17, No.13, September, 1971.

28. Herdt R.W. and E.A. Baker, "Agricultural Wages production and the High Yielding Varieties", *Economic and Political Weekly,* Vol. 7, No.13, March 25, 1972.

29. K. Singh, "The Impact of New Agricultural Technology of Agricultural Wage Rates and Employment in IADP Districts", *Indian Journal*

of Agricultural Economics, Vol. 27, No.4, October-December, 1972.

30. K. Bardhan, "Factors Affecting Wage Rates for Agricultural labour", *Economic and Political Weekly,* Vol. 8, No. 26, June 30, 1973.

31. S.M. Pandey, "Wage Determination in Indian Agriculture : An EmpiricalAnalysis", *Indian Journal of Industrial Relations,* Vol. 9, No. 1, July 1973.

32. Indira Hirway, "Trend in Agricultural Wages in Gujarat", *Indian Journal of Agricultural Economics,* Vol. 28, No. 3, July-September, 1973.

33. Rajinder Sondhi and Karam Singh, "Impact of High yielding Varieties on Agricultural Wages in Punjab", *The Indian Journal of Agricultural Sciences,* Vol. 44, No. 1, January, 1974.

34. A.C. Gangwal and Paramatma Singh, "Impact of Green Revolution on Farm Labour", *Eastern Economist,* Vol. 62, No. 21, May 24, 1974.

35. D.K. Grover and K.N. Rai, "Effects of the Agricultural Revolution on theAgricultural and Industrial Labour in Haryana", *Indian Journal of Agricultural Economics,* Vol. 29, No. 3, July-September, 1974.

36. R.K. Pandey and U.N. Dixit, "Inter-Temporal Analysis of Productivity and Wages of Farm Labour in Ferozepur district (Punjab)", *Indian Journal of Agricultural Economics,* Vol. 29, No. 3, July-September, 1974.

37. M.L. Singh and K.K. Singh, "Factors Determining Agricultural Wages : A Study", *Indian Journal of*

Agricultural Economics, Vol. 29, No. 3, July-September, 1974.

38. Gupta, J.R., "An Inter-Regional Study Into the Seasonality of Agricultural Wage Rates with Particular Emphasis on its Relationship with the Levels of Employment", *Indian Journal of Agricultural Economics,* Vol. 29, No. 3, July-September, 1974.

39. Chawla, J.S., "Impact of Green Revolution on Employment, Earnings and Wage Rates (A case Study in District Amritsar)", *Indian Journal of Agricultural Economics,* Vol. 29, No. 3, July-September, 1974.

40. B. Bhuyan and Chakraverty, "A Study of Wages and Income in Rural Areas of Orissa", *Indian Journal of Agricultural Economics,* Vol. 29, No. 3, July-September, 1974.

41. Raju, V.T., "Impact of Green Revolution on Wages and Incomes of Hired Labour in IADP District, West Godavari", *Indian Journal of Agricultural Economics,* Vol. 29, No. 3, July-September, 1974.

42. Deepak Lal, "Agricultural Growth, Real Wages and the Rural Poor in India", *Economic and Political Weekly,* Vol.6, No.26, June, 1976.

43. Rohini Nayyar, "Wages of Agricultural Labourers in Uttar Pradesh", *Economic and Political Weekly,* Vol. 11, No. 45, November 6, 1976.

6

Area Profile

A. Government vide its G.O.Ms. No. 168 Revenue RA-1 Department dated 19.04.2002 have ordered merger of Perambalur & Ariyalur District as perambalur District with Head quarters at perambalur with effect from 19.04.2002.

B. District Profile At a Glance

1. Geographical Area	: 3691 sq. km.
No. of Blocks	: 10
No. of Taluks	: 6
2. No. of Villages	: 347
3. Rainfall :	Normal 996.5
Actual:	1998: 1239.30
	1999: 1176.82
	2000-2001: 517.00
	2001-2002: 605.50
4. Agriculture (Ha)	
a. Geographical area:	369137

b. Net shown area	:	215554	
c. Fallow land	:	47648	
d. Land not available for cultivation	:	58546	
e. Cultivable waste	:		9272
5. Irrig..tion (Ha)			
a. Gross Irrigated area	:		72309
b. Net Irrigated Area	:		66772
c. By Canals	:		10196
d. By Tanks	:		6670
e. By wells	:		34755
f. Bore well	:		15068
g. Other	:		83
6. Size of holdings		No.	Area (ha)
a. Less than 1 ha	:	206728	87559
b. Between 1 and 2 ha	:	47810	68118
c. Above 2 ha	:	27728	94548
7. Animal husbandry			
a. Plough animals		87410	
b. Dairy animals (1997)			
i. Cows		290335	
ii. Buffaloes		78641	
iii. Sheep		84622	
iv. Goat		271692	
v. Poultry		374397	
8. Population (Provisional-2001 Census)			
a. Male		588441	
b. Female		592588	

c. Total 11,81,029

9. Classification of Workers

a. Cultivators 239760

b. Agricultural labourers 250244

c. Non-Agricultural labourers 122170

10. The area under major Crops are furnished below:

Paddy	48734
Cotton	18396
Groundnut	35997
Sugarcane	12673
Millets & Others Cereals	34748
Pulses	3442

11. SSI Permanent Registration No. of Units During 2002-2003

Sl. No.	*No. of Units*	*Line of Activity*	*Investment in Plant & Machinery*	*Investment in Land & Building*	*Capacity Rs. in lakhs*	*Employment*
1	32	Rice Milling, flour milling, paddy hulling	4761	9047	11907	101
2	5	Ice Candy	2597	500	2776	88
3	106	Readymade Garments & Tailoring	566	2385	2849	125
4	12	Wooden Furniture	409	558	510	16
5	14	Stitching of Leather Chappals	37	158	245	15
6	13	Tube, Tyre vulcanizing	276	383	701	22
7	14	Fabrication of gates & grills	579	575	1374	36
8	7	Desk Top Publishing	1763	685	635	15
9	2	Book-Binding	33	135	66	4
10	1	Spray painting	15	10	36	2
11	1	Biochemical Testing	90	19	75	1

12	61	Repairing & servicing of637 Automobile two wheelers		1912	1815	76
13	15	Xerox, Job Typing	509	938	558	23
14	2	Black & White photo Film Processing	21	39	42	2
15	1	Rewinding of Yarn	100	150	225	1
16	11	Blue Metal Crushing	1741	1229	2020	56
	297	Total	14,134	18,723	25,835	583

a. Industrial Scene

The industrial activity is mostly centred around the large cement units and in the tiny sector, Handloom units, in Jayankondam area. In recent times quarrying (the mining) has picked up. Except Perambalur all the blocks have been declared as industrially backward. Efforts are now being taken to set up an Industrial Estate near Perambalur town.

b. Major Food/Commercial/Plantation Crops

Paddy, Groundnut, Sugarcane and Millets are the major crops in the district. During the last 13 years area under cotton cultivation has expanded substantially. Cashew is the major plantation crop occupying 24,000 ha of land. Coriander and chillies are the horticulture widely cultivated.

Development Programmes in Perambalur District

New Schemes at a Glance

Some new areas are made available to the banks for financing, the gist of which is given below:

Financing Farmers for Purchase of Land for Agricultural Purpose (NABARD circular No. DPD-FS/152001-02 dated 20 August 2001)

The scheme aims at providing term finance to small and marginal farmers including share croppers and tenant cultivators to purchase agricultural land as well as fallow and wasteland to develop and cultivate it with a view to increasing production and productivity. Small and marginal farmers who own maximum of 5 acres of non-irrigated land or 2.5 acres of irrigated land including purchase of land under the scheme and share croppers/tenant farmers are eligible. Complete details of the project proposal of the farmer should be obtained by the bank while considering finance for purchase of land. The margin will be 20% and the land purchased out of bank finance and mortgaged in favour of the bank will form the security. The repayment period will be 7-10 years including a maximum moratorium period of 24 months. The project cost may include cost of land, value of stamp duty, registration charges for sale/mortgage deed and other land development expenses. During the period of the loan, the farmer is not expected to sell the land.

Financing for Setting up of Agri Clinic and Agri Bussiness Centers by Agriculture Graduates (NABARD Circular DPD-FS/12/2001-02 dated 23 July 2001)

The Scheme aims at supplementing the existing extension network to accelerate the process of technology transfer to agriculture, providing supplementary sources of input supply and services and providing gainful employment to agriculture graduates in new emerging areas in agricultural sector. The scheme is open to Agriculture graduates/Graduates in subjects allied to agriculture like horticulture, animal husbandry, forestry, dairy, veterinary, poultry farming, pisciculture and other allied activities either individually or on joint/group basis. Agriclinics are envisaged to provide expert services and advice to farmers on cropping practices, technology dissemination, crop protection from pests & diseases, marker trends and prices of various crops in the markets and also clinical services for animal health etc. which, would enhance productivity of crops/animals. Agribusiness centres are envisaged to provide input supply, farm equipments on hire and other services.

Construction I Renovation I Expansion of Rural Godowns (NABARD Circular No. 92/ICD 20/2002-03 dated 12 April 2002)

The scheme aims at creation of scientific storage capacity with allied facilities in rural areas to meet the requirements of farmers for storing farm produce, processed farm produce, consumer articles and agricultural inputs and there by preventing, distress sale immediately after harvest. Known as 'GRAMIN BHANDARAN YOJANA', the scheme has provisions to meet the farmers' immediate financial requirements through pledge loans from banks without being compelled to sell the produce at a time when prices are low. The project can be taken up by individuals, farmers, group of farmers/growers, Partnership / Proprietary firms, NGOs, SHGs, Companies, Corporations, Co-operatives, Agro processing cooperative societies, Agriculture Produce Marketing Committees, Marketing Boards and Agro processing Corporations. Renovation / Expansion of rural godown will however be restricted to godowns constructed by cooperatives only.

Kisan Credit Card

To enable the cultivating farmer get the financial requirement in time and at require quantum, Govt. of India introduced Kisan Credit Card Scheme. The farmers are provided with a credit card by the financing bank and based on the crops cultivated, the drawing limit is fixed. The limit may include some additional amount for consumption purpose also. The card allows flexibility to the farmer regarding number of drawals, quantum, etc. which will result in reduction of interest burden. The borrowers are eligible for insurance cover under Personal Accident Insurance Scheme. The premium amount of Rs. 15 per annum will be borne by the farmer and the financing agency at the ratio 1:2. The indemnity amount will be Rs.25,000 or Rs.50,000 depending on the nature of loss.

Rural Employment Generation Programme (Gramodyog Rozgar) by KVIC: (NABARD Circular No.131 DPD-NFS 13/2002 dated 11 June 2002)

REGP is implemented through KVIC with a view to generate employment in rural area, to develop entrepreneurial skill among rural employed youth and to achieve the goal of rural industrialization. The beneficiaries will be individuals, Institutions/Co-op. Societies/Trusts/Regd. Companies and Self Help

Groups. Regarding financing SHGs under REGP, the eligible SHGs will be identified by Banks/NABARD with the help of NGOs and they will be provided EDP training in recognized training institutes of NABARD/Banks/Training centres of KVTC. Cost of training shall be shared by NABARD and KVIC. It need not be insisted that the group should take up group enterprises. However, group enterprises may be considered only when the group voluntarily comes for the same.

The following Government Sponsored Programmes are continuing as Poverty Alleviation Programmes: Swarnajyanthi Grama Swarozgar Yojna (SGSY)

This rural poverty alleviation programme is implemented through DRDA with an aim of lifting at least 30% of the BPL above poverty line in the next 5 years and to ensure that the swarozgaris get a net income of Rs. 2000 per month in the next 3 years. More emphasis is given for group activity.

Prime Ministers Rozgar Yojna (PMRY)

The Self Employment Programme for educated youth is implemented through District Industries Center. Those who have completed VIII standard, within the age of 35 years (for selected categories including women 45 years) and having a family income of less than Rs. 40,000 are covered under the scheme. The beneficiaries can undertake self employment activity though bank credit and they are eligible of 15% subsidy subject to a maximum of Rs. 7,500.

THADCO Schemes

With a view to lift the standard of living of SC/ST, THADCO is implementing various schemes with bank loan component. The beneficiaries will be getting subsidy assistance from THADCO.

Annual Credit Plan 2003-2004

Perambalur District at a Glance

Sector-wise Allocation

SECTOR	AMOUNT IN CRORES	% OF SHARE
Agriculture	160.89	80.43
Industries	8.94	4.47
Services	30.20	15.10
Total	200.03	100.00

Agency-wise Allocation

Agency	*Amount in Crores*	*% of Share*
Commercial Banks	132.67	66.33
Co-operative Banks	67.36	33.67
Total	200.03	100.00

Perambalur District (Performance Uunder SGSY Scheme 2002-2003)

(Rs in lakhs)

Sl.No.	*Particulars*	*Target*		*Achievement*	
		Physical	*Financial*	*Physical*	*Financial*
1	Individuals	300	25.50	454	36.12
2	Revolving Fund	94	9.40	164	16.40

3	Economic Activities	300	221.79	179	205.64
	TOTAL	694	256.69	797	258.16

Performance Under THADCO 2002-2003

(Rs in lakhs)

Sl.No.	*Particulars*	*Target*		*Achievement*	
		Physical	*Financial*	*Physical*	*Financial*
1	Individuals	164	49.00	164	49.00
2	Revolving Fund	184	46.00	184	46.00
3	Economic Activities	25	77.26	25	77.26
	TOTAL	373	172.26	373	172.26

7

Economic Analysis

Distribution of Sample Households

The sample agricultural labour households have been classified into two categories, the house holds with land and the households without land. The households with land are further classified into three categories:

1. households possessing up to 1 acre of land;
2. those who possess between 1 and 2 acres of land; and
3. households who have more than 2 acres of land.

Out of the total 240 sample households, 149 households (62.08%) possess land and the landless labour sample households constitute 91 (37.92%). Among the sample households with land, 22.08 percent households possess less than 1 acre, 19.17 percent possess between 1 and 2 acres and 20.83 percent possess above 2 acres. The above data reveals that majority of agricultural labour households are either landless or possess small extent of land.

The sample agricultural labour households have

been classified into five categories on the basis of average income of the household. They are the households with an annual income of less than Rs. 3,000; households who earn an average income between Rs. 3000-6000; households with an annual income in the range of Rs. 6000-9000; the households with an annual income in the range of Rs. 9000-12,000; and lastly the households who have an income of above Rs. 12,000.

The Table shows that as much as 44.17 percent of the sample households fall in the income range of Rs. 6000-9000 whereas, the households whose annual income falls in the group of Rs. 3000-6000 constitute 35.00 percent. The households who earn an average income between Rs. 9000-12,000 constitute 17.50 percent of the sample households. The data show that 80 percent of the sample households have an income of less than Rs.9000 per year.

Distribution of Sample Agricultural Labour Households by Income Levels

Sl. No.	*Income Levels*	*Number of Households*	*Percentage to Total*
1.	Below Rs.3,000	3	1.25
2.	Rs.3,000-6,000	84	35.00
3.	Rs.6,000-9,000	106	44.17
4.	Rs.9,000-12,000	42	17.50
5.	Above Rs.12,000	5	2.08
	Total	240	100.00

The sample agricultural labour households have also been classified into four categories according to size of the family.

Distribution of Sample Agricultural Labour Households by Size of the Family

Sl. No.	*Size of the Family (in persons)*	*Number of Households*	*Percentage to Total*
1.	Up to Two	17	7.08
2.	3 and 4	108	45.00
3.	5 and 6	103	42.92
4.	7 & Above	12	5.00
	Total	240	100.00

The Table reveals that 45.00 percent of the households possess an average family size of 3-4 members whereas 42.92 percent of the households have on an average 5-6 persons per household. The average size of the family in the sample households works out of 4.45 persons.

The Table shows that as much as 75.83 percent of the sample households belong to Scheduled Castes and Scheduled Tribes, whereas 15 percent of the sample households belong to Backward Castes and 9.17 percent of the sample households belong to other castes. The Table reveals that majority of the sample agricultural labour households are from Scheduled Castes and Scheduled Tribes.

Castewise Distribution of Sample Agricultural Labour Households

Sl. No.	*Caste*	*Number of Households*	*Percentage to Total*
1.	Scheduled Caste/Scheduled Tribes	182	75.83
2.	Backward Castes	36	15.00

3.	Other Castes	22	9.17
	Total	240	100.00

Age and Sex Composition

The total population of the sample households is 1067 persons of which males account of 544 (50.98%) and females for 523 (49.02%). The age composition pattern of the sample population reveals that 35.24 percent are in the age group of (0-14) years, 24.09 percent in the age group of (14-30) years and 22.30 percent in the age group of (30-45) years. The persons in the age group of (45-60) years and 60 and above years account for 11.38 percent and 4.69 percent respectively. The table reveals that about 60 percent of the sample population is in the age of active economic participation.

Age and Sex Composition of the Population in the Sample Households

Sl. No.	Age Group	Male Number of Persons	Male Percentage	Female Number of Persons	Female Percentage	Total Number of Persons	Total Percentage
1.	0-14	187	34.38	189	36.14	376	35.24
2.	14-30	118	21.69	139	26.54	257	24.09
3.	30-45	127	23.35	111	21.22	238	22.30
4.	45-60	82	15.07	64	12.24	146	11.38
5.	60 & Above	30	5.51	20	3.82	50	4.69
	Total	544	100.00	523	100.00	1067	100.00
		(50.98)		(49.02)			(100.00)

Note : Figures in parenthesis denote percentage to total.

Working Status

According to 1981 Census, main workers are those who have worked or engaged in any economically productive activity for a major part of the year or more than six months during the reference year. Marginal workers are those who have worked less than six months during the reference year. Non-workers are those who have not worked in any productive activity at any time during the reference year. According to the above definition, the population in the sample households has been classified into main workers, marginal workers and non-workers.

It is observed from the Table that out of 1067 persons in the sample households, main workers constitute 43.58 percent and marginal workers 7.69 percent. Non-workers account for 48.73 percent of the population. In the landless households, 48.65 percent of the population are main workers, 7.26 percent are marginal workers whereas 44.09 percent are non-workers. Among the households who possess land, non-workers (51.22%) outnumber main workers (40.86%) and marginal workers (7.92%). This clearly shows that,

Working Status of the Population in the Sample Households

Sl. No.	Category	Male Number of Persons	Male Percentage	Female Number of Persons	Female Percentage	Total Number of Persons	Total Percentage
Landless Households							
1.	Main Workers	107	56.32	74	40.66	181	48.65
2.	Marginal Workers	4	2.10	23	12.64	27	7.26

3.	Non-Workers	79	41.58	85	46.70	164	44.09
	Total	190	100.00	182	100.00	372	100.00
Households with Land							
4.	Main Workers	161	45.48	123	36.07	284	40.86
5.	Marginal Workers	17	4.80	38	11.14	55	7.92
6.	Non-Workers	176	49.72	180	52.79	356	51.22
	Total	354	100.00	341	100.00	695	100.00
Total							
7.	Main Workers	268	49.26	197	37.67	465	43.58
8.	Marginal Workers	21	3.86	61	11.66	82	7.69
9.	Non-Workers	225	46.88	265	50.67	520	48.73
	Grand Total	544	100.00	523	100.00	1067	100.00

The percentage of non-workers is more in the sample households with land than the landless. On an average, the non-workers constitute nearly 50 percent of the population. The non-working population among females is more than that of males in the sample households.

Working Status of Population in the Sample Households by Income Levels

Sl. No.	*Income Levels*	*Working Status*			*Total*
		Main Workers	*Marginal Workers*	*Non-Workers*	
1.	Below Rs. 3,000	3 (42.86)	—	4 (57.14)	7 (100.00)
2.	Rs. 3,000-6,000	156 (47.13)	13 (3.93)	162 (48.94)	331 (100.00)
3.	Rs. 6,000-9,000	213 (44.56)	36 (7.53)	229 (47.91)	478 (100.00)
4.	Rs. 9,000-	84	27	114	225

	12,000	(37.33)	(12.00)	(50.67)	(100.00)
5.	Above	9	6	11	26
	Rs. 12,000	(34.61)	(23.08)	(42.31)	(100.00)
	Total	465	82	520	1067
		(43.58)	(7.69)	(48.73)	(100.00)

Note : Figures in parenthesis denote percentage to total.

The Table reveals that there are 7 persons in the first income category of which 3 are main workers and 4 non-workers. In the second income category, out of 331 persons, 47.13 percent are main workers, 3.93 percent are marginal workers and 48.94 percent are non-workers. Main workers constitute 44.56 percent of the 478 persons belonging to the income group of Rs. 6,000-9,000 while the non-workers constitute 47.91 percent. Main workers account for 37.33 percent of the population in the income group of Rs. 9,000-12,000 and 34.61 percent in the last income group. A close examination of the table shows chat there is gradual decline in the ratio of main workers with the increase in the income group from the second category onwards while there is gradual increase in the percentage of marginal workers with the increase in family income. On the whole, out of the sample population, main workers account for 43.58 percent, marginal workers for 7.69 percent and the non-workers for 48.73 percent.

Literacy Status

Literacy Status of the Population in the Sample Households

Sl. No.	Education Levels	Male Number of Persons	Male Percentage	Female Number of Persons	Female Percentage	Total Number of Persons	Total Percentage
1.	Illiterates	251	46.14	355	67.88	606	56.80
2.	Primary Education	159	29.23	113	21.61	272	25.49
3.	Secondary Education	121	22.24	54	10.32	175	16.40
4.	Higher Education	13	2.39	1	0.19	14	1.31
	Total	190	100.00	182	100.00	372	100.00

Note : Literates exclude children in the age group 0-6 who are treated as illiterates.

The Table reveals that 56.80 percent of the total population are illiterates. The percentage of literates among males constitutes 53.86 percent whereas the percentage of literates among females constitute 32.12 percent.

Literacy Status of the Population in the Sample Households by Income Levels

Sl. No.	Income Levels	Literacy Status: Illiterates	Literacy Status: Literates	Total
1.	Below Rs. 3,000	4 (57.14)	3 (42.86)	7 (100.00)
2.	Rs. 3,000-6,000	187 (56.50)	144 (43.50)	331 (100.00)
3.	Rs. 6,000-9,000	275 (57.65)	202 (42.35)	477 (100.00)
4.	Rs. 9,000-12,000	129 (57.08)	97 (42.92)	226 (100.00)

5.	Above Rs. 12,000	11	15	26
		(42.31)	(57.69)	(100.00)
	Total	606	461	1067
		(56.79)	(43.21)	(100.00)

Note : Figures in parenthesis denote percentage to total.

The Table reveals that the percentage of illiterates is more than that of literates in all the income size groups except the top income group having an average income of more than Rs.12,000.

Marital Status

The Table reveals that married persons account for 50.23 percent while 43.86 percent are unmarried. There are 265 married persons, 259 unmarried persons and 20 widowers among the males constituting 48.71 percent, 47.61 percent and 3.68 percent of the total male population respectively. There are 271 married persons, 209 unmarried persons and 43 widows among the females constituting 51.82 percent, 39.96 percent and 8.22 percent of the total female population respectively.

Marital Status of the Population in the Sample Households

Sl. No.	*Marital Number*	*Male Number of Persons*	*Male Percentage*	*Female Number of Persons*	*Female Percentage*	*Total Number of Persons*	*Total Percentage*
1.	Married	265	48.71	271	51.82	536	50.23
2.	Unmarried	259	47.61	209	39.96	468	43.86
3.	Widow/Widower	20	3.68	43	8.22	63	5.91
	Total	544	100.00	523	100.00	1067	100.00

Land Holdings

Land Holdings of the Sample Households (in acres/in Rs.)

Sl.	Particulars	Size Group (in acres) (0-1)	(1-2)	Above 2	Total
1.	No. of Households	53	46	50	149
2.	Irrigated Land	2.50	15.29	30.95	48.74
3.	Unirrigated Land	24.81	28.30	64.88	117.99
4.	Uncultivable Land	1.10	1.00	1.30	3.40
	Total	28.41	44.59	97.13	170.13
5.	Average Per Household	0.50	0.97	1.94	1.14
6.	Average Per Capita	0.11	0.22	0.43	0.25
7.	Total Value	3,19,350	5,65,700	10,29,250	19,14,300
8.	Average Value Per Household	6,025.47	12,297.83	20,585.00	12,847.65
9.	Average Value Per Capita	1,223.56	2,746.12	4,514.24	2,754.39

The sample households possess 170.13 acres of land. Out of the total land, the households in Group I possess 28.41 acres, households in Group II possess 44.59 acres and households in the last group possess 97.13 acres. The total value of the land has been estimated at Rs.19,14,300 and the average value of land per household works out to Rs.12,847.65. The per capita value of land is worked out to Rs.2,754.39. The table reveals that though some households possess land, they get marginal returns from those lands and hence depend more on wage employment in agriculture to take out their livelihood.

Land Utilisation

Out of the 160.53 acres of gross cropped are, the

households in Group I possess 25.91 acres (16.41%), households in Group II possess 43.67 acres (27.20%) and households in the last group (above 2 acres) possess 90.95 acres (56.66%). The net area sown of the sample households is worked out to 152.68 acres and the area sown more than once to 7.85 acres. Most of the farms have no irrigation facilities. During rainy season, groundnut crop is raised as a rainfed crop whose production mostly depends on the rainfall which is uncertain.

Land Utilisation of Farms of Sample Households (in acres)

Sl. No.	*Size Group*	*Net Area sown*	*Area Sown more than once*	*Gross Cropped Area*	*Perce-ntage*
1.	0-1	25.61	0.30	25.91	16.14
2.	1-2	40.37	3.30	43.67	27.20
3.	Above 2	86.70	4.25	90.95	56.66
	Total	152.68	7.85	160.53	100.00

Cropping Pattern

Cropping Pattern in the Farms of Sample Households (in acres)

Sl. No.	*Crops*	*Size Group (in acres)* (0-1)	*(1-2)*	*Above 2*	*Total Area*	*Percen-tage*
Irrigated						
1.	Groundnut	0.20	3.30	5.75	9.25	5.76
2.	Sugarcane	—	3.10	3.55	6.65	4.14
3.	Paddy	2.60	10.60	23.55	36.45	22.71
	Unirrigated					
4.	Groundnut	23.11	26.67	58.40	108.18	67.39
	Total	25.91	43.67	90.95	160.53	100.00

The principal crops grown in the farms belonging to sample households are paddy, sugarcane and groundnut. Table reveals that out of the 160.53 acres of gross cropped are irrigated goundnut was raised in 9.25 acres (5.76%) paddy in 36.45 acres (22.71%), and sugarcane in 6.65 acres (4.14%). Rainfed groundnut covered an area of 108.18 acres. The above data shows that the sample households mostly possess dry land and they grow groundnut under rainfed conditions.

Irrigation

The Table reveals that the sample agricultural labour households have a gross irrigated are of 47.05 acres. The net irrigated area is worked out to 39.50 acre, and the area irrigated more than once to 7.55 acres. Out of the 47.05 acres of gross irrigated area, the households in Group I possess 2.50 acres (5.31 percent), Group II households possess 16.50 acres (35.07%) and households in the last group of above 2 acres possess 28.05 acres (59.62%). The gross irrigated are accounts for 29.31 percent of the gross cropped area.

Irrigated Area of Farms of Sample Households (in acres)

Sl. No.	*Size Group Group*	*Net Irrigated Area*	*Area Irrigated More than Once*	*Gross Irrigated Area*	*Percentage*
1.	0-1	2.50	—	2.50	5.31
2.	1-2	13.20	3.30	16.50	35.07
3.	Above 2	23.80	4.25	28.05	59.62
	Total	39.50	7.55	47.05	100.00

Housing

Particulars of Housing of the Sample Households

Sl. No.	Particulars	Landless Households	Households with Land	Total
1.	Cost of Construction (in Rs.)	152990	451180	604170
2.	Average Cost Per Households (in Rs.)	1681.21	3028.05	2517.38
3.	No. of Houses Inherited	51	80	131
4.	No. of Households Received Assistance from the Government for House Construction	11	22	33
5.	Quantum of Assistance (in Rs.)	30,350	1,23,000	1,53,350
6.	Average Per Household (in Rs.)	2,759.09	5,590.91	4,646.97

Among the 240 sample households, 131 households had dwelling houses constructed by the ancestors whereas 109 households constructed the houses on their own. The total cost of construction has been worked out to Rs.6,04,170 and the average per household to Rs.2,517.38. Out of the total sample households 33 households received financial assistance from the government to the extent of Rs.153,350 and the average per household is worked out to 4,646.97. From the above, it is to conclude that most of the sample agricultural labour households have not availed financial assistance from the Government for constructing the houses.

Among the 240 households 162 houses (67.50%) have thatched roof, 47 houses (19.58%) have tiled and

22 houses (9.17%) have R.C.C. roof and only 9 houses (3.75%) have asbestos roofing. The above data reveals that majority of the sample households still live in thatched houses and they have no pucca houses.

Particulars of Type of the Houses of the Sample Households

Sl. No.	*Types of the Houses*	*Landless Households*	*Households with Land*	*Total*	*Percentage to total*
1.	Thatched	69	93	162	67.50
2.	Tiled	13	34	47	19.58
3.	Asbestos	4	5	9	3.75
4.	R.C.C.	5	17	22	9.17
	Total	91	149	240	100.00

Livestock

The Table reveals that the total value of livestock in the sample households is worked out to Rs.3,31,666. The average value of livestock per household is worked out to Rs. 1,381.94 and the per capita value Rs.310.84. The landless households on an average possess livestock worth of Rs. 1,160.52 per household and the average value per capita is worked out to Rs. 283.89. The households with land on an average possess livestock worth of Rs. 1,517.17 per household and the average value per capita is worked out to Rs. 325.27.

The Table reveals that there is no trend in one direction in the average value of livestock across different income groups The highest average value per household is worked out for the households included in the income group of Rs. 9,000-12,000 at Rs. 2673.83 and the lowest value is recorded by the income group of Rs.3,000-6,000. The average value of livestock per capita is the highest at Rs.524.29 for the lowest income group.

Estimated Value of Livestock in the Sample Households by Income Levels

Sl. No.	*Income Levels*	*Total Value*	*Average Per Household*	*Average Per Capita*
1.	Below Rs. 3,000	3,670	1,223.33	524.29
2.	Rs. 3,000-6,000	46,756	556.62	141.62
3.	Rs. 6,000-9,000	1,59,464	1,504.38	333.61
4.	Rs. 9,000-12,000	1,12,301	2,673.83	499.12
5.	Above & 12,000	9,475	1,895.00	364.42
	Total	3,31,666	1,381.94	310.84

Farm and Household Assets

Among the household assets, the dwelling houses account for 79 percent of the total value of household assets. The average value of household assets per household has been worked out to Rs.3,848.71 for the households with land as against the average value of for the landless households Rs. 3,173.25. On the whole the average value of household assets is worked out to Rs. 2,067.29.

The Table shows that the average value of farm and household assets per household has increased with the increase in the income of the household. The average per capita assets has also increased with the increase in the income level except in the case of the households in the income range of Rs. 9000-12000.

Estimated Value of Farm and Household Assets of Sample Households by Income Levels

Sl. No.	*Income Levels*	*Total Value*	*Average Per Household*	*Average Per Capita*
1.	Below Rs. 3,000	4,092	1,364.00	584.57
2.	Rs. 3,000-6,000	2,13,776	2,544.95	645.85
3.	Rs. 6,000-9,000	3,64,711	3,440.67	762.99
4.	Rs. 9,000-12,000	1,56,239	3,719.98	694.40
5.	Above & 12,000	22,763	4,552.60	875.50
	Total	7,61,581	3,173.25	713.76

The total estimated value of assets of sample households is Rs. 10,93,247. The average value of assets per household is worked out to Rs. 4,555.20 and the average value of per capita to Rs. 1,024.60. The average value of assets per household and per capita is higher in households with land than that of the landless.

Estimated Value of Total Assets of Sample Agricultural Labour Households

Sl. No.	*Assets Levels*	*Total*	*Landless Household*	*Households with land*
1.	Household and Farm Asset			
	Total Value	188123.00	573458.00	761581.00
	Average Per Household	2067.29	3848.71	3173.25
	Average Per Capita	505.71	825.12	713.76
	Percentage	64.05	71.73	69.66
2.	Livestock			
	Total Value	1,05,607.00	2,26,059.00	3,31,666.00
	Average Per Household	1,160.52	1,517.17	1,381.94
	Average Per Capita	283.89	325.27	310.84

	Percentage	35.95	28.27	30.34
3.	Total			
	Total Value	2,93,730.00	7,99,517.00	10,93,247.00
	Average Per Household	3,227.80	5,365.89	4,555.20
	Average Per Capita	789.60	1,150.38	1,024.60
	Percentage	100.00	100.00	100.00

The Table gives the average value of assets per households and per capita of the sample households in different income groups. The average value of assets per household is Rs. 4,555.20, and it has increased with the increase in the income levels. The average per capita value of assets is estimated at Rs. 1024.60.

8

Employment and Wages

Factors Influencing the Employment

The employment pattern of agricultural labourers is influenced by several factors. The employment of agricultural labourers depends on the size of land holdings of the cultivators in the sample villages. If the size of the land holdings is small, the demand for hired labour will be low and if the size of the land holdings is high, the demand for hired labour will be high. The employment of agricultural labourers depends on demand and supply of labourers, If the supply of labour is high, unemployment prevails in the village. If the supply of labour is low, employment position of the labour will be favorable and demand for labour is felt. It is observed that the influence of caste on the employment opportunities is negligible in the sample village.

Irrigation facilities influence the period of demand for labour. If irrigation facilities are available throughout the year, the demand for labour will be there throughout the year. In areas where agriculture depends mainly on rainfall, labour is not needed when the rainy season is over. Assured irrigation facilitates the farmers to grow several varieties of crops throughout the year which will ultimately result in the increase of employment opportunities for the agricultural labourers. In the study area, river irrigation is totally absent. In Erpedu mandal, small canals and wells are the sources of irrigation while, in Gangavaram and Gudipala mandals, major source of irrigation is wells. Dry land constitutes a significant area under cultivation on which groundnut is raised as a rainfed crop during rainy season only. Cultivated area influence the demand for labour in the sense that if more land is brought under cultivation, there will be more demand for labour and hence helps to increase the employment opportunities of agricultural labourers.

Farm mechanization and technology are assumed to have significant influence on the employment in the sense that when certain activities are mechanized, the demand for labour for those activities decreases. For example, if there is tractorization, the demand for labour ploughing and land levelling will fall to a considerable extent. The high yielding varieties are assumed to have increased the employment potential of the labourers since it calls for frequent application of water, fertilizers, pesticides and also requires more weeding, large volume of transportation, better transplantation, scientific farming, sowing and other improved agricultural operations. All these operations require more labour.

The demand for certain type of labour varies from crop to crop. The demand for female labour is low when compared to male labour in extensive sugarcane growing areas. The activities including ploughing, plantation, irrigating, manuring and sugarcane cutting and jaggery making operations need mostly male labour. But in extensive rice growing areas, the demand for female labour is high compared to male labour. The demand for labour also varies from operation to operation. Certain operations would require hard manual labour which can not be undertaken by the aged people.

Types of Employment

Agricultural labourers can be broadly divided into two categories i.e., attached labourers and casual labourers.

Attached labourers are attached to specific landlords for a specified period. Agricultural labourers who have been regularly employed on some contract or on some particular understanding during the most part of a year and are paid wages per annum are considered as attached labourers. They have to work only on the farms of the employer cultivator. In addition to working on the farm, they are often to do some non-agricultural work for the landlord's family. The contracts of attachment with a particular employer for specified period have been done on oral understanding in the study area. It is observed that written contracts are totally absent in the study area.

Agricultural labourers who have not been in continuous employment and who have not been working for a single landlord all the days during the period of investigation and have also been working irregularly in the past, seasonally or annually are considered as casual labourers. Casual labourers can be divided into two categories i.e., landless casual labourers are those casual labourers who do not possess any land and who are purely depending on wage paid agricultural employment. Unlike attached labourers, they have to face the problem of seasonal unemployment. The advantage of casual labourers over attached labourers is that they get more wages, if work is available throughout the year. The landed labourers are those who possess some land holdings. In addition to working on their own farms, they work for wages also for most of the days in a year. There are 547 agricultural labourers in the sample households of which 15 persons are attached labourers and the remaining 532 persons are casual labourers.

Employment by Category

Table presents the average person days employed by sample labourers during the reference year. The table reveals that the labourers in the sample households have worked for 1,37,539 person days of which they have engaged in agricultural work for as much as 68.69 percent of the person days. Nonagricultural work accounts for 9.43 percent and the sample labourers are employed in their own work for 21.88 percent of the person days. On an average the employment of Labourers per household works out to 573.08 person days and the per capita employment to 258.53 person days in a year. There is no significant difference between the pattern of employment of labourers between the households with land or landless. This is due to the fact that majority of households possess small pieces of land, mostly unirrigated. They grow only groundnut in the rainy season and they depend more on wage paid employment to make out their livelihood. Only very few households possess small extent of lad under irrigation. Landless casual labourers I the sample households worked for 50,787 person days of which they have engaged in agricultural work for as much as 71.63 percent of the person days worked. Non-agricultural work accounts for 10.10 percent and they are employed in their own work for 18.27 percent of the person days. On an average the employment of labourers per household works out to 558.10 person days and the per capita employment to 257.80 person days in a year. The labourers with land in the sample households worked for 86,752 person days of which they have engaged in agricultural work for as much as 66.98 percent of the person days worked. Non-agricultural work accounts for 9.03 percent and the sample labourers are employed in their own work for 23.99 percent of the person days. On an average the employment of labourers per household works out to 582.23 person days and the per capita employment to 258.96 person days in a year.

Employment (in person days)

Sl. No.	*Category*	*Total*	*Average Per Household*	*Average Per Capita*	*Percentage to Total*
Landless Households					
1.	Agricultural Labour	3638	399.76	184.66	71.63
2.	Non- Agricultural Labour	5129	56.36	26.03	10.10
3.	Self-Employment	9280	101.98	470.11	18.27
	Total	50787	558.10	2570.80	100.00
Households with Land					
4.	Agricultural Labour	58103	389.95	173.44	66.98

5. Non-Agricultural Labour	7834	52.58	23.39	9.03
6. Self-Employment	20815	139.70	62.13	23.99
Total	86752	582.23	258.96	100.00
All Households				
7. Agricultural Labour	94481	393.67	177.59	68.69
8. Non- Agricultural Labour	12963	54.01	24.37	9.46
9. Self-Employment	30095	125.40	56.57	21.88
Grand Total	137539	573.08	258.53	100.00

Employment of Sample Agricultural Labourers the Sample Mandals

Employment (in person days)

Sl. No.	*Mandals*	*Total*	*Average Per Household*	*Average Per Capita*	*Percentage to Total*
	Gudipala				
1.	Agricultural Labour	32800	410.00	185.31	71.04
2.	Non- Agricultural Labour	4835	60.44	27.32	10.47
3.	Self-Employment	8537	106.71	48.23	18.49
	Total	46172	577.15	260.80	100.00
	Erpedu				
4.	Agricultural Labour	31184	389.80	171.34	66.06
5.	Non- Agricultural Labour	4359	54.49	23.95	9.24
6.	Self-Employment	11661	145.76	64.07	24.70
	Total	47204	590.05	259.36	100.00
	Gangavaram				
7.	Agricultural Labour	30497	381.21	176.28	69.06
8.	Non-Agricultural Labour	3769	47.11	21.79	8.53
9.	Self-Employment	9897	123.72	57.21	22.41
	Total	44163	552.04	255.28	100.00

	All Mandals				
10.	Agricultural Labour	94481	393.67	177.59	68.69
11.	Non-Agricultural Labour	12963	54.01	24.37	9.43
12.	Self-Employment	30095	125.40	56.57	21.88
	Grand Total	137539	573.08	258.53	100.00

Table shows the average person days employed by sample labourers in the sample mandals during the reference year. In Guidipala mandal, the sample labourers have worked for 46,172 person days of which they were engaged in agricultural work for as much as 71.04 percent of the person Non-agricultural work account for 10.47 percent and the sample labourers are employed in their own work for 18.49 percent of the person days. On an average the employment of labourers per household works out to 577.15 person days and the per capita employment to 260.86 person days in the reference year. In Erpedu mandal, the sample labourers are engaged for 47,204 person days of which they have engaged in agricultural work for as much as 66.06 percent of the person days worked. Non-agricultural work accounts for 9.24 percent and the sample labourers are employed in their own work for 24.70 percent of the person days. On an average the employment of labourers per household and per capita employment works out to 590.05 person days and 259.36 person days in the reference year respectively. In gangavaram mandal, the total employment of sample labourers is worked out to 44,163 person days of which agricultural work accounts for 69.06 percent ad non-agricultural work for 8.53 percent, the sample labourers are employed in their own work for 22.41 percent of the person days. On an average the employment of labourers per household and per capita works out to 552.04 person days and 255.28 person days in the reference year respectively. The data reveals that the average person days employed is higher though marginally in Erpedu followed by Gudipala and Gangavaram. This shows that employment is positively associated with irrigation.

9

Findings, Suggestions and Conclusion

Sample Design

The sample households for the study have been selected based on three stage random sampling method. The study covers Chittoor district of Andhra Pradesh. All the mandals in the district have been divided into three categories, developed, developing and less developed on the basis of some selected economic indicators. Erpedu, Gudipala and Gangavaram mandals representing the above three categories have been selected as the first stage units of sampling. The villages in each selected mandal have been classified into five groups on the basis on the percentage of agricultural labourers to main workers. From each mandal, five villages were selected representing all the five groups. From each selected village, agricultural labour households have been classified on the basis of land owned and landless. The sample households have been chosen in probability proportion to the existing households under each category. On the whole, the study covered covered 240 sample households. Out of the 240 sample households. 91 households are landless and the remaining 149 households possess land. Among the 149 households with land, 53 households possess less than 1 acre, 46 households possess land or 1 to 2 acres and 50 households possess land of above 2 acres. Agricultural labour households have been selected on the basis of income criteria. The households which earn 50 percent of more of their annual income from agricultural wages have been considered as agricultural labour households.

Sample Households

Out of the 240 sample households covered in the study, 62.08 percent possess some lad most of which is dry land and uneconomic. The landless labour households constitute 37.92 percent of the total sample. The sample households have been classified on the basis of their gross income. Majority of the households (44.17%) earn an annual income of Rs. 6,000-9,000 per annum while 35 percent of the households earn between Rs 3,000 and Rs. 6,000. About 17.50 percent have their annual income in the range of Rs. 9,000-12,000. This shows that most of the most of the households, on an average, have an income of less than Rs. 9,000 per annum. The average size of the family is worked out to 4.45 persons. Among the sample households, as many as 75.83 percent of the households belong to Scheduled Caste and Tribes and 15.00 percent belong to Backward Classes. The other castes account for 9.17 percent. This shows that most of the agricultural labourers hail from the Scheduled Castes and Tribes.

The total population of the sample households is

1,067 persons of which main workers constitute 43.58 percent and marginal workers 7.69 percent. The non-workers account for 48.73 present of the population. As many as 56.80 percent of the population in the sample households are illiterates. Out of the 240 sample households, 149 households have ownership of 170.13 acres of lad of which 28.65 percent is irrigated, 69.35 percent unirrigated and 2.00 percent uncultivable land. The average lad per household works out to 1.14 acres and the average value per household works out to Rs. 12,847.65 The sample households reported a net sown area of 152.68 acres and a gross cropped area of 160.53 acres. Rainfed groundnut occupied 67.39 percent of the gross cropped area followed by paddy covering 22.71 percent,irrigated groundnut with 5.76 percent and sugarcane with 4.14 percent of the total cropped area.

Out of the 240 sample agricultural labour households 67.50 percent live in thatched houses and 19.58 percent live in small houses with tiled roofs. The sample households possess milch animals, poultry birds, sheep, goats, etc. The average value of livestock per household has been worked out to Rs. 310.84. The average value of farm and households assets per household and per capita has been estimated at Rs 3,173.25 and Rs. 713.76 respectively.

Employment

The employment pattern of agricultural labourers depends on several factors like size of lad holding, supply of labour, irrigation, crop pattern, level of technology, age and sex composition of labour force etc. In the sample households, there are 547 casual agricultural labourers and 15 attached labourers. The results of the study reveal that a casual agricultural labourer is employed in agricultural operations as hired labour for 177.59 person days and in non-agricultural work for 24.37 person days. A casual labourer is said to have engaged in self-employment for 56.57 person days. On the whole a casual labour is employed for 258.33 person days in a year on an average No significant variation is observed in the average number of person days employed between the three mandals covered by the study. The average number of person days employed per household has been worked out to 573.08 person days in a year.

An analysis of the pattern of employment of sample labourers by income levels reveals that the proportion of non agricultural and self–employment has increased with the increase in the income level. The average person days employed per household is on the increase with the increase in the size of income. There is no relation in one direction between average per capita employment and income level. On the whole it is fair to conclude that there is no significant impact of the income level on the pattern of employment among agricultural labour households.

Employment of agricultural labourers depends upon the type of crops grown in the respective regions. Groundnut, paddy and sugarcane are the principal crops n the study area. An analysis of employment of sample labourers by crop reveals that groundnut has accounted for 37.71 percent of the person days employed by the sample labourers closely followed by paddy with 35.78 percent and sugarcane accounting for 22.95 percent. Groundnut is the principal crop and it is raised mostly as a rainfed crop. In few pockets, groudnut is raised as an irrigated crop mostly during rabi season. The employment in this crop depends upon rainfall and seasonal conditions. On the contrary, paddy is raised under wells and it utilizes labour intensively compared to groundnut. The growing of paddy is restricted depending upon the availability of water. Sugarcane is a perennial crop requiring labour use at different levels throughout the year. Sugarcane crop is widely grown in the central part of the district and in some eastern parts of the district. Thus employment conditions of agricultural labourers is determined by type of crops which depends on irrigation facilities. Regarding operation wise employment, harvesting, and threshing operations provide employment for 42.37 percent of the total person days employed by the sample labourers followed by weeding and sowing/transplantation accounting for 23.49 percent and 22.26 percent of the person days employed respectively.

The results of the study show that in recent times agricultural operations are completed in time by utilization of labour on contract basis. The results show that the sample labourers are employed on contract basis for 39.69 percent of the person days employed. The agricultural labourers formed into a group enter into contract with the owner cultivator for the completion of some specific job. They usually work for longer hours and complete the work in time and they get usually higher remuneration. The sample labourers have reported that they have worked on piece rate basis for 12.04 percent of the person days. This is mostly practiced in the case of harvesting of groundnut in the study area. The sample labourers are observed to have worked on daily wages for 48.27 percent of the total person days employed.

The trends in season-wise employment indicate that the sample labourers are employed for more number of person days during *kharif* season. In the study area, the crops are raised mostly during the *Kharif* season, since the area under crops during the *Rabi* season, since the area under crops during the Rabi season depends upon the availability of water in the wells. The sample labourers are employed for 72.30 percent of the total person days employed in *Kharif* season while the Rabi season provided employment for 27.70 percent. Sugarcane and mulberry are the perennial crops remaining throughout the year. The analysis of sex-wise and crop-wise employment reveals interesting trends. On the whole, a casual male labourer is employed on an average for 180.92 person days as against 174.07 person days in the case of female labour. Regarding the sex-wise person days employed per household, male labourers are observed to have worked for 206.55 person days as against 187.12 person days in the case of female labourers. Regarding crop-wise utilization of labour it is observed that female labourers have accounted for more person days of employment in the case of paddy and sericulture whereas male labourers dominate in the case of groundnut and sugarcane. Sugarcane provides employment more to male labourers. This is to conclude that sex-wise employment is determined by type of crops ad nature of agricultural operations in the concerned region.

On an average, the sample labourers are employed in non-agricultural work for 24.37 person days in a year. Regarding the employment of attached labourers, they have worked for 291.27 person days in a year. They have been employed in agricultural operation for 215.93 person days and non–agricultural work for 38.20 person days. An attached labourer is observed to have engaged in self-employment for 37.14 person days. The attached labourer remained unemployed for 73.73 person days in a year on an average.

An attempt has been made to analyse the reasons for absenteeism. In the case of casual labourers, the labourers remain unemployed for106.47 person days on an average of which they remain unemployed for 50.52 percent of the person days for want of work and the remaining days due to festivals, sickness, bad weather, etc. In the case of labourers, they were employed for 45.66 percent of the person days absent for want of work. The hours of work are determined by traditions in the concerned areas and also by nature of agricultural operations.

Wages

Wages constitute the main source of income of agricultural labourers. The wages of agricultural labourers are influenced by several factors like type of agricultural production, seasonal factors, type of operations, supply and demand for labour, local traditions, age and sex composition of labourers, *etc.* Agricultural labourers are paid wages on daily basis or yearly basis. Casual labourers are paid on daily basis and attached labourers on yearly basis. Wages are usually paid in cash, in kind or partly in cash and partly in kind. Wages are also paid on piece rate basis. For contract labour, the amount will be paid for completing the operation to the entire group as per the agreement and the amount will be shared by the labourers themselves. Wages are mostly paid in kind, particularly during the harvest of crops like paddy and other food crops. In the case of commercial crops wages are generally paid in cash.

Wage rates vary from operation to operation and from place to place. In Gudipala manda, labourers are paid at the rate of Rs.15 per day and for other operations Rs.10 per day in addition to provision of meal in the afternoon. For harvesting of sugarcane and jaggery preparation, higher wages of Rs.15 per day is paid. In Erpedu manda Labourers are paid at the rate of Rs. 10 per day and for harvesting of sugarcane and paddy, they are paid more. For certain other operations they are paid at Rs. 8 per day. In Gangavaram mandal, for all operations, labourers are paid at the rate of Rs. 8 per day and for ploughing, they are paid Rs. 10 and for harvesting the wage rate varied from Rs. 12-15. For almost all the operations, except harvesting of groundnut, agricultural labourers are provided with one meal in the midday.

Income

The average income per household of the sample households has been worked out to Rs. 6,871.49 from all sources. The average income of landless households is estimated at Rs. 6,133.40 as against Rs. 7,322.27 per household for households with land. Higher average income for households with land may be due to crop income. Out of the average income from all sources, agricultural wages alone constitute 61.34 percent while the income from non-agricultural sources accounts for 11.08 percent, income from crops for 12.49 percent, income from milk production for 8.01 percent and income from other livestock for 6.24 percent. For landless households, agricultural wages account for 71.95 percent of the total average income. The corresponding percentage for households with land stood at 55.92 percent. The sample households with land could earn Rs. 1,382.29 per household from crop production on an average. Therefore, agricultural wages constitute major source of income for all the agricultural labour households though some households who possess land derive some income from the lands also.

Expenditure

The average per household expenditure of the sample households has been estimated at Rs.5,590.79 per year. The expenditure of the sample households who are landless is worked out to Rs.5,175.04 as against Rs. 5,844.71 for the households with land. For the sample households, as much as 46.86 percent of the expenditure is spent on food, while clothing accounts for 8.61 percent, tobacco for 5.74 percent, social ceremonies for 5.14 percent and alcohol for 4.90 percent. A comparison of the expenditure pattern of landless households with that of the households with land reveals almost the similar trend. The average expenditure per households is the highest at Rs.5,694.40 in Gudipala mandal followed by Erpedu with Rs. 5,597.79 and the lowest expenditure of per household of Rs.5,480.19 has been is recorded by Gangavaram mandal.

Among all the categories of sample households, food constitutes the major item of expenditure. The sample households are observed to have spent meagre amount on education and assets. The average per capita expenditure is estimated at Rs.1,257.54. The average expenditure per household has increased with the income level of the family. The percentage of expenditure on food in the size of the income of the household. The average expenditure on food per household has increased with income level of the family. The percentage of expenditure on food in the total expenditure has increased with the increase in the income up to a certain level and afterwards it is gradually declining though it accounts for a major share in total expenditure.

Savings

The results of the study reveal that only 33.75 percent out of the 240 sample households have reported savings outstanding at the beginning of reference year. The average savings per household and per capita have been worked out by taking into consideration only the reported households.

The average savings outstanding at the beginning of the reference year has been worked out to Rs.1,068.27 per household and Rs.243.75 per capita. There is no significant difference in the savings of landless households and households with land and among the three selected mandals. Among the sample households 73.33 percent have reported that they had savings during the reference year. The average savings per reported household and per capita during the reference year stood at Rs. 1,746.40 and Rs. 384.21 respectively. The average savings per household during the reference year are estimated at Rs. 1,865.74 for households with land as against Rs. 1,503.62 for landless households.

The average savings per household are the highest in Gudipala mandal at Rs.2,674.53 followed by Erpedu and Gangavaram with Rs.1,301.75 and Rs.1,120.64 respectively. There is a positive relation between average savings and the income level of the household as the average savings per household has increased with the increase in the size of income. The above data shows that the savings of the sample agricultural labour households are very low.

Indebtedness

The results of the study show that as many as 67.92 percent of the sample agricultural labour households are indebted. The average figures for debt has been calculated by taking into consideration only the indebted households not all the households. The average debt outstanding of the sample households at the beginning of the reference year has been worked out to Rs. 2,290.50 per reported household and Rs. 508.03 per capita. The average outstanding debt of the households with land stood at Rs. 2,546.15 as against Rs. 1,840.68 for landless households. Out of the outstanding debt, the sample households owe 43.70 percent of their debt to institutional agencies, 28.41 percent to the cultivators and 11.52 percent to professional moneylenders. This shows that agricultural labourers in the study area depend more on institutional sources. The households who possess land have more access to institutional credit than the landless households ass revealed by the percentage of debt from institutional sources. The data on source-wise outstanding debt of the sample households income levels show that the higher income groups have more access to institutional credit than the lower income brackets.

The analysis of purpose-wise debt shows that the sample households have become indebted mostly to meet the expenditure of social functions like marriages, for the purchase of milch animals and for consumption purposes. The sample households with land have reported that they have borrowed to meet the crop expenditure, and some households have reported debt due to purchase of pumpsets and land.

Poverty

Poverty among the sample agricultural labour households has been measured on the basis of Seventh Plan estimate of Rs. 1,280 per capita and Rs. 6,400 per household per annum. As per this estimate, 28.59 percent of the sample persons are observed to be living below the poverty line. The percentage of poor persons among the landless is higher at 40.05 percent than among the persons with land with 22.45 percent living below the landless is higher at 40.05 percent than among the persons with land with 22.45 percent living below the poverty line.

Sen's "P" measure is concerned not merely with the number of people below the poverty line but also with the amounts by which the incomes of the poor fall short of the specified poverty line. The higher the short fall from the poverty level, the greater the incidence of poverty.

The results of the poverty measure on the basis of per capita income, suggest that poverty measure is estimated at 0.029 for the sample households on the whole. The results also reveal that the incidence of poverty is higher in the backward and unirrigated areas than the developed and irrigated area as the value of "P" is more at 0.035 in Gangavaram mandal when compared to 0.024 in the case of Gudipala mandal. The analysis shows that the incidence of poverty is more in the case of low income groups than the higher income groups.

On the basis of per capita expenditure, percentage of persons below the poverty line is the highest at 73.91 percent in Gudipala mandal followed by Gangavaram mandal with 55.82 percent and Erpedu with 51.61 percent. The incidence of poverty is more in Gudipala than the other two mandals.

No specific trend in one direction in the percentage of persons below the poverty line and the value of "P" measure across different income groups on the basis of per capita expenditure is observed. The above analysis shows that the incidence of poverty depends on the assets, proportion of irrigated area, crop pattern and cropping intensity in the concerned region.

Conclusions

Majority of agricultural labourers belong to Scheduled Castes. Most of them are landless or possess small pieces of land which are unirrigated and uneconomic. They have neither good housing nor adequate assets which generates income. They remain unemployed for more than 100 days in a year on an average. The employment of agricultural labourers depends on the nature of crops, irrigation and size of holdings in the concerned regions. The conditions of employment of attached labour are observed to be more secured and remunerative than the casual labourers.

The average wages of the agricultural labourers are low. The average income of most of the agricultural labour households is just above the poverty line. The average expenditure of the agricultural labour households is low and a major share of expenditure has been spent on food. The savings are reported to be low and 67.92 percent of the households have reported that they are under debt. On the basis of income, 29 percent of the sample persons are still living under poverty line and on te basis of capita expenditure more than 60 percent of the persons are living below the poverty line.

Since the modern industrial sector in India is not in a position to absorb even the urban unemployed, the surplus labour in the agricultural sector have to be productively utilized by evolving suitable strategies which would generate off-farm and non-farm employment in rural areas. Agricultural labourers particularly landless labourers are to be assisted n such a way creating income generating assets which would improve their economic position and in turn labour productivity. The improvement in the economic conditions of the agricultural labourers, the large segment of work force would promote economic welfare in general and ultimately would promote economic welfare in general ad ultimately lead the Indian economy on the path of growth with stability.

Bibliography

Acharya, S.S., Green Revolution and Farm Employment, *Indian Journal of Agricultural Economics*, Vol. 28,No. 3, July–September,1973.

Agarwal, A.N., *Indian Agriculture and its Problems*, Ranjeet Printers & Publishers, Delhi, 1953.

Agarwala, N. "Disguised Unjemployment, Unlimited Suppplied Labour and the Wage gap", *Indian Economic Journal*, Jan. March, 1972.

Ahuja, H.C., Labour Absorption Problem and india's Development Strategy, *The Indian Journal of Labour Economics*, Vol. 34, No. 4, Oct-Dec, 1991.

Anne Boothe, R.M., Sundrum, Labour Absorption in Agriculture, *Theoretical Analysis and Empirical Investigations*, Oxford University Press, Delhi, 1984.

Anuva Saika, State of Female Agricultural Labour in Assam, *Kurukshetra*, Vol. 32, No. 6, March, 1984.

Bagi, F.S., "Economic Development with Surplus Labour: A Welfare Criterion", *Indian Economic Journal*, July, 1980.

Bansal, P.C., *Agricultural Problems of India*, Vikas

Publishing House (Pvt.) Ltd., Delhi, 1975.

Bardhan, Factors Affecting Wage, Rates for agricultural Labour, *Economic and Political Weekly,* Vol. 8, No. 26 June 30, 1973.

Bariroch, P. *Urban Unemployment in Developing Ceuntries: The Nature of the Problem and Proposals for its Solution,* ILO, Geneva, 1973.

Basu, Timir. "Calcutta's Sandal Makers", *Economic and Political Weekly,* Aug. 6, 1977.

Beinfeld, M. "The Informal Sector and Peripheral Capitalism: The Case of Tanzania", *Institute of Development Studies Bulletin,* Vol. 6, 1975.

Beinfeld, M. and M. Godfrey. "Measuring Unemployment and the Informal Sector: Some Conceptional and Statistical Problems", *Institute of Development Studies Bhulletin,* Vol. 7, 1973.

Bell, C.L.G. (Ed.). "The Informal Sector and Marginal Groups", *Bulletin of Institute of Development Studies,* Vol. 5, No. 2/3, 1973.

Chaubey, Improving The Lot of Landless Labourers, *Kurukshetra,* Vol. 23, No. 7, January 1, 1975.

Chopra. D.S., *The Minimum Wages Act, 1948,* Eastern Law House, Calcutta, 1981.

Dandekar, V.M. and N. Rath, *Poverty in India,* Indian School of Political Economy, Pune, 1971.

Dantwala, M.L. *Poverty in India: Then and now,* Macmillan Company of India, Delhi, 1973.

Fonseca, A.J.,(ed), *Challenge of Poverty in India,* Vikas Publications, Delhi, 1972.

Gangwal and Parmatma Singh, Impact of Green Revolution on Farm Labour, *Eastern Economist,* Vol. 61, No. 21, May 24, 1974.

Governent of India, The Seventh Five Year Plan, 1985-90, Planning Commission, New Delhi, Ocotober, 1985.

Hardyal Singh, Socio-Economic Conditions of Agricultural Labour in Ludhiana, *Kurukshetra*, Vol. 22, No. 33, Septempber, 1974.

Hicks, J.R., *The Theory of Wages*, McMillan & Co. Ltd., London, 1964.

Indira Hirway, Labour Absorption in the Indian Economy Some Issues, *The Indian Journal of Labour Economics*, Vol. 34, No. 4, October-December, 1991.

International Labour Organisation, *Employment Expansion in Indian Agriculture*, Bangkok, 1979.

Jorgenson, D., The Development of a Dual Economy, *Economic Journal*, Vol. 71, 1961.

Khusro, A.M., *Readings in Agricultural Development*, Allied Publishers Private Limited, Bombay, 1968.

Kindleberger P. Charles, *Economic Development*, The McGraw-Hill Book Company, New York, 1958.

Lewis, W.A., *Economic Development with Unlimited Supplies of Labour*, The Manchester School of Economics and Social Studies, May, 1954.

Lorenzo, A.M., *Agricultural Labour Conditions in Northern India*, New Book & Company, Bombay, 1964.

Madan, B.K., *Aspects of Economic Development and Policy*, Allied Publishers Private Limited, Bombay, 1964

Mamoria, C.B., *Agricultural Problems of India*, Kitab Mahal, Allahabad, 1973.

Nanvathi, Manilal, B. & Anjaria, J.J., *The Indian Rural Problem*, Indian Society of Agricultural Economics, Bombay, 1970.

Narayan Parasad Sharma, Wage Differentials for Women

Agricultural Labourers, *Yojana,* Vol. 33 No. 12, July 1-15, 1989.

Pramit Chaudhuri, *The Indian Economy: Poverty and Development,* Vikas Publishing House Pvt. Ltd., New Delhi, 1978.

Pramit Chaudhuri (ed), *Readings in Indian Agricultural Development,* London: George Allen & Unwin Limited, 1972.

Randhawa, M.S., *Green Revolution A Case Study of Punjab,* Vikas Publishing House Pvt. Ltd., Delhi, 1974.

Rao, V.K.R.V. (ed), *Agricultural Labour in India,* Asia Publishing House, New Delhi, 1962.

Sen, A.K., *Choice of Techniques,* Basil Blackwell, Oxford, 1960.

Sen, A.K., *Employment, Technology and Development,* Oxford University Press, Delhi, 1975.

Thorner, Daniel & Alice, *Land and Labour in India,* Asia Publishing House, Bombay, 1961.

Theodor Bergmann, Problems of Mechanization in Indian Agriculture, *Indian Journal of Agricultural Economics,* Vol. 18, No. 4, October-- December, 1963.

Umananda Phukan, Employment and Earnings of Agricultural Labour in Assam, *Indian Journal of Agricultural Economics,* Vol. 29. No. 3, July-September, 1974.

Usha Rao, N.J., Female Labour Participation Rates Among Scheduled Castes of Karnataka, *The Indian Journal of Labour Economics,* Vol. 21, No. 1 & 2, April-July, 1978.

Verma, R.C., Farm Mechanisation and Labour use, *Eastern Economist,* Vol. 67, No. 26, January, 1978.

Vijendra Kabra, Census of Female and Child Labour in Rural India, *The Indian Worker,* Vol. 30, No. 1, October 7, 1981.

Vijay Nayak, Shailaja Prasad, On Levels of Living of Scheduled Castes and Scheduled Tribes, *Economic and Political Weekly,* Vol. 19, No. 30, July 28, 1984.

Vyas, V.S., Agricultural Labour in Four Villages, Some Observations, *Khadi Gramodyog,* Vol. 11, No. 5, February, 1965.

Vyas V.S., *Agricultural Labour in Four Indian Villages,* Sardar Patel Agro-Economic Research Centre, Vallabh Vidyanagar, Gujarat, 1964.

Vyas, V.S. and G. Mathai, Farm and Non-Farm Employment in Rural Areas: A Perspective for Planning, *Economic and Political Weekly,* Vol. 13, No. 6-7, Annual Number, 1978.

Index